BARNES

AN AMERICAN ENTERPRISE

An 1835 woodcut of Bristol, Connecticut, viewed from the general area where the first Barnes factory was built. In the background are Federal Hill and the Congregational Church.

BARNES

AN AMERICAN ENTERPRISE

By Ogden Tanner

■

WITH AFFECTION AND RESPECT

WE DEDICATE THIS BOOK

TO THE MEN AND WOMEN OF BARNES GROUP—

PAST, PRESENT AND FUTURE.

■

_____
Carlyle F. Barnes

_____
Wallace Barnes

BARNES: AN AMERICAN ENTERPRISE

Author and Picture Editor:
Ogden Tanner
New Canaan, Connecticut

Design and Production:
Leonard Wolfe Design Associates, Inc.
Westport, Connecticut

Printing:
Eastern Press, Inc.
East Haven, Connecticut

Published by Barnes Group Inc.
123 Main Street, Bristol, CT 06010

Library of Congress Catalog Card No. 91-077300

COVER: *The company's factory, circa 1860.*

CONTENTS

APPENDICES

INTRODUCTION

THE LAST THING THE WORLD NEEDS IS another dull corporate history, the kind that nobody reads. In researching this project, however, I soon discovered that the cast of characters was anything but dull. How can you *not* get interested in a company that was started by an amiable Yankee opportunist and jack-of-all-trades, the first Wallace Barnes—who bankrolled it with the grand sum of $1,600 he got from selling a wagonload of hoop-skirt wire?

Even more remarkably, led by a succession of Wallace's descendants, the company is alive and kicking 134 years later, which can't be said about many companies that began more than a century ago. What happened during those years offers a rare glimpse into American business history—and not a few lessons in corporate survival. It also says something about the durability of old-fashioned values in a changing society. As one Barnes employee put it: "It may sound corny, but this company really *cares* about the things it makes, and about the people who make them. Working here you're not just a number. You're a member of a family."

What follows, then, is a sort of corporate family album, a scrapbook of the extended family that Barnes has become—and, with any luck, will continue to be for another century or more.

Associated Spring Corporation

The changing company logo, from a pre-1920 version through the one that is in use today.

CHAPTER ONE

YANKEE TRADER

An 1860 advertisement of the Dunbar-Barnes partnership.
The hoop-skirt springs were made in "Crinoline Hall," the building at far left.

*Wallace Barnes, manufacturer of clock springs.
Commenced business in 1857. Building, 2 stories; situated
about one-quarter mile south of depot. Employs 20 hands.
Uses an 11 horse power turbine wheel.*

— WEBB'S N.E. RAILWAY AND MANUFACTURER'S STATISTICAL GAZETTEER, 1869.

The year 1857 was a momentous, if uncertain, one in which to be born as a company.

James Buchanan was taking office as the 15th President of the United States, whose total population, largely confined to the Eastern half of the nation, had yet to reach 30 million. Elisha Otis

An early tintype of the company's founder, Wallace Barnes, posing for the photographer in his Sunday best.

was installing the first passenger elevator; amateur clubs were forming the beginnings of organized baseball; the first transatlantic cable was being laid. Connecticut was becoming a state of industrial legends, including Samuel Colt, who, in a huge new armory he had built in Hartford, was turning out 250 of his famous revolvers every day.

His guns, and many others, would be used all too soon. Since the Supreme Court's Dred Scott decision in March, which inflamed tensions between North and South, storm clouds had been gathering for the Civil War.

Meanwhile Bristol, Connecticut, a bustling town of some 3,000 souls southwest of Hartford, was making industrial history itself. Over the past half century, along with neighboring villages, Bristol had become the clock-making capital of America, thanks to Seth Thomas, Elias Ingraham, Eli Terry, Chauncey Jerome, Joseph Ives and others who manufactured timepieces for sale everywhere around the country that itinerant salesmen and their wagons could reach.

Until the early 1800s clocks had been custom made and relatively expensive, using all-wooden movements powered by weights. Gradually, however,

Bristol clock makers developed models that could be mass produced from standardized parts and powered by springs, which were made first of tempered brass and later of steel. In so doing, they laid the foundations for the American spring-making industry.

A more immediate effect was to put clock prices within the reach of even the humblest home. By the mid-1840s an English traveler to the hinterlands was able to report that "in Kentucky, Indiana, Illinois, Missouri, and here in every dell of Arkansas where there was not a chair to sit on, there was sure to be a Connecticut clock." The notorious "Yankee peddler" earned much of his reputation for shrewdness in such situations. He would set a clock running in the home of a wary customer, assuring him that it was only "on trial." By the time he returned on his rounds, most families found it impossible to give up their newfound luxury. The salesman thereupon collected, if not in scarce cash, then in mules, horses, furs, chickens or anything else he could trade.

In those hardscrabble days, individual entrepreneurs came and went with astonishing regularity, if not from ordinary financial reverses then from disastrous fires that consumed their tinderbox plants. Like many American towns, moreover, Bristol was feeling the effects of a widespread business depression, the "Panic of '57," which took more than the usual toll. One of many firms to go under that year was A. S. Platt & Company, a small manufacturer of clocks and clock springs that had recently started making wire hoops for hoop skirts, or "crinolines," the latest fashion craze.

Among Platt's dozen or so employees was a genial 29-year-old named Wallace Barnes, whose ancestors had lived in the Bristol area for more than 200 years (see page 9). Born on Christmas Day, 1827, and nicknamed "Bub," he had grown up near the corner of South and Main Streets, where both his grandfather Thomas and his father Alphonso had their homes as well as a family hotel and a general store, the latter specializing in clocks in addition to drugs and general merchandise.

Wallace worked in the store for a while, becoming knowledgeable as a druggist, but after frequent disputes with his father moved north to the village of Winsted, taking along Eliza Jane Fuller as his bride, where he ran his own druggist's shop for two years. Persuaded to return to the family business, he came back to Bristol but apparently had another falling out. This time he decided to try his hand in the clock-making trade, contracting to cut glass for clock doors and supply parts of movements for several firms, including Edward L. Dunbar and A. S. Platt.

When the Platt firm went bankrupt, Wallace Barnes was earning the princely sum of $1.25 a day. The owner could not come up with back wages in cash, offering instead to pay off his obligations in kind. Barnes took his share of the settle-

A classic Bristol clock, made by Birge & Fuller around 1845, used a wagon-type spring at the bottom to keep it running for 30 hours. Part of the extensive collection at Bristol's American Clock and Watch Museum, its Gothic "steeple" style was first introduced by another Bristol clockmaker, Elias Ingraham, whose family company made popular clocks and pocket watches until the 1960s.

ment in hoop-skirt wire.

What happened next is the stuff of corporate legends. While some of the details are sketchy, to say the least, Wallace Barnes emerges as one of the greatest Yankee traders of all time.

Barnes, it seems, loaded his precious wire onto a wagon and set out for Albany, where it is likely that Platt had previous dealings with the owner of a

the farm for a blacksmith shop on School Street operated by one "Hop" Holt (whether Hop forsook his horseshoes to become a prominent Missouri agriculturalist is not known). Since Barnes didn't much like blacksmithing either, he found a buyer for the smithy who was willing to pay $1,600 in cash, a handsome sum in those days.

And, with his newfound purchasing

Fancy letterhead of the Dunbar Company, with the founder's portrait and some of its wares.

haberdashery store. Strapped for cash himself by the depression, the owner agreed to swap his store for the wire, which could readily be made into fast-selling hoops. Since Barnes had no desire to take up retailing in Albany, he looked around for another purchaser. Within a few days he had swapped the haberdashery store—for a farm in Missouri, sight unseen.

When he got back to Bristol, the resourceful Barnes, with a little more wheeling and dealing, managed to trade

power, what did Wallace Barnes do? He bought the donor of his original load of wire, A. S. Platt.

Included in the bill of sale, which came to $1,513.30—plus a $500 payment to the seller for agreeing to abandon springmaking in Bristol for five years— were spring winders, a forming machine, a slitting mill, two rolling barrels, one press, 22 cords of pine wood and 4,500 pounds of coal, plus various finished and unfinished springs and a supply of raw material in the form of cast steel sheets.

Dunbar employees outside their factory in the 1880s. A large bell in the tower, rung each night at 9 o'clock, sounded curfew for younger Bristol residents until halfway into the 20th Century.

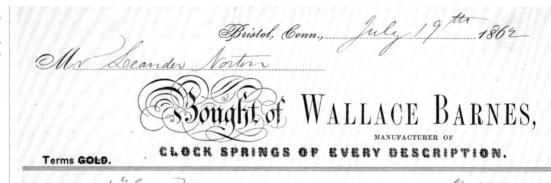

Along with the lot, Barnes apparently acquired an ace in the hole: a secret method of tempering steel springs by heating them and quenching them in oil. He hastened to make a written agreement with five key employees that anyone revealing the process would forfeit $1,000, a precaution that seems to have kept things under wraps. At the same time he brought in his younger brother Thomas as an employee. He also wisely teamed up with E. L. Dunbar, a more experienced Bristol manufacturer and an old family friend, the partners putting in $2,000 each toward operating expenses and the purchase of more equipment. Considering the returns they were to realize in a few short but glorious years, it was money well spent.

By early 1858 Barnes and Dunbar were making springs and hoops for their own account near the corner of South and Main Streets, in a small, two-story building adjacent to the site on which the company's Bristol factory stands today.

The next year, when the boom in crinolines reached fever pitch, the partners began building a nearby structure they christened "Crinoline Hall" (which, after the rage for hoop skirts subsided, long served as Bristol's town hall and public auditorium). The "Hall" was a long, odd-looking shed with an arched, open first story where cordwood was stored, and an enclosed second floor were the wood was burned in portable furnaces used to temper the steel wire for hoops. To meet the mounting demand, Dunbar and Barnes put their work force—which had exploded to more than 150—on three eight-hour shifts around the clock, six days a week, a practice unheard of at the time. The highest wage paid to a skilled worker, company

A LONG AND COLORFUL HERITAGE

While the Barnes Group as a business had its beginnings in 1857, the roots of the Barnes family—now in its 12th generation in Bristol—go back two centuries earlier, providing an unusual vignette of American history on a personal scale.

Thomas Barns (the "e" was not added until the fifth generation) arrived from England around 1630, and for his services in the Pequot War received an allotment of land in Hartford, later moving to Farmington where his property overlapped what is now the Bristol line. Though he was a staunch churchgoer, his wife Mary, who had borne him three children, was caught up in the widespread witch hunting of the day, convicted of "entertaining familiarity with Satan" and put to death by hanging in 1662. Not only did Thomas lose his wife; he had to pay the Hartford jailkeeper 21 shillings in fees for the time she spent in his care.

By his second wife, also named Mary, Thomas had two children, the second of whom, Ebenezer, in 1728 became the first permanent settler of Bristol, then known as New Cambridge; the father of 15 children, he was also the town's first tavernkeeper, serving brew made from the barley he grew on his farm. His son Stephen, in addition to farming, had a half interest in a gristmill and a sawmill and was a leading deacon of Bristol's Congregational Church. Stephen's son Thomas engaged in tinsmithing and served as a soldier in the Revolution, fighting the British at the Battle of White Plains.

The most remarkable of the early line was Thomas Barnes, Jr., who became Bristol's largest retailer, not only operating a general store, but sending his trading wagons for months at a time as far as the banks of the Mississippi and the Gulf of Mexico. He was also the town's major distiller, shipping his brandy around the state, and a leading private banker, real estate developer, town official and pillar of the family church. At one time or another he manufactured carriages, owned a button shop and headed his own clock-making firm, Thomas Barnes, Jr. & Company, which made brass-movement clocks. When death came in 1855 at the age of 82, he left an estate

Home built by Thomas Barnes, Jr., on South Street in Bristol.

valued at $64,000, a substantial sum for those days.

Wallace Barnes, the company's founder, undoubtedly inherited some of his trader's blood from his grandfather Thomas, as well as an independence of spirit from his father, who stands out as a maverick in the family line. Alphonso Barnes, who lived from 1804 to 1877, not only had a distinctively un-Yankee name, but, as family biographer George W. Hull put it, "departed frequently from approved New England standards of conduct."

Unlike his predecessors, all Congregationalists of the stern, Calvinist mold, Alphonso became a prominent advocate of Spiritualism, a liberal new doctrine that

made many converts in Bristol. He loved hunting and riding, taking great pride in his dogs and horses, and often loaded his boat on a wagon for the trip out to Lake Compounce, where he would spend long, lazy days, alone or with friends, fishing for pickerel, bass and perch. He also had a fondness for liquor, although he was hardly an exception in that era. Spirited drinking was common among the menfolk. The ladies, too, liked to bring out the brandy on occasion, especially on wash days, to ease their tasks.

A dashingly handsome man, Alphonso was strongly attracted to women, and in fact had five wives. The first was Almira Andrews, whom he married in 1825 when he was 21; she bore him Wallace and four other children before her death in 1840 at the age of 35. He then wedded a 17-year-old, Mary Ely, who died three years later; his third marriage, to the widow Mary Hinman, also ended with her death in six years after bearing him a daughter and a son. Two more marriages, to Caroline Tuttle and Maria Dutton, were equally short-lived, terminating in divorce.

Like his father, and many of his contemporaries, Alphonso experimented freely in the business world. Ventures in the family carriage-making trade, and in clock manufacturing with Andrew Jerome, both ended in failure. More successful was his administration of his father's general store, which he expanded under

CONTINUED

the name of Alphonso Barnes & Sons, though frequent clashes with his son Wallace led the latter to set up shop on his own in Winsted for a while.

Among Bristolites, Alphonso is best remembered for two notable additions to the town. One was the old Bristol House, which used to stand at the corner of South and Main, a genial hotel and tavern that Alphonso built in 1834 and ran for many years. A center of Bristol's social life, it was the scene of regular dances, some of which, a town historian appreciativelly noted, "reached the dignity of balls."

Alphonso's other contribution was the Bristol Fire Depart-

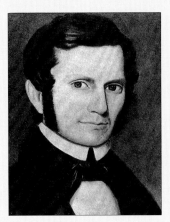

Alphonso Barnes

Thomas Barnes, Jr.

ment, which he and Colonel E. L. Dunbar, who was to become his son's partner, organized in 1853 to fight the frequent fires that devastated wooden homes and factories. They raised $2,000 by subscription to build an engine house for a hand pump, a wagon and 500 feet of leather hose, manned by a company of 60 volunteers. Alphonso's son Wallace, a later fire commissioner, helped persuade the town to buy two newer pumpers powered by steam. The tradition is proudly carried on today by Wallace's great-grandson, Carlyle ("Hap") Barnes, who has been a fire buff, and Bristol fire commissioner, for much of his adult life.

records reveal, was 18 3/4 cents an hour. Women, who constituted the bulk of the payroll, mostly braiding and finishing the skirt frames for sale in New York City, generally made 5 cents.

The heyday of the joint venture was recalled by Dunbar's son, Edward B. Dunbar, who went to work for the company at the age of 18:

"The hoops were packed in barrels and shipped each day to New York. The firm had a branch of the factory there at Murray Street and employed 200 girls in finishing the skirts for the retail market. The output of the Bristol factory was very much larger than the New York branch could finish up, and the major portion of each shipment was sold to the concerns that made a business of finishing the skirts.

"Every morning there was a scramble for the barrels when unloaded at the Murray Street office. There were always two or three men after each barrel and, of course, only one could buy. Mr. Dunbar said that he always sold to the man who was sitting on the barrel."

In 1859 the partners' total sales amounted to an impressive $224,817— $30,807 in clock springs and $194,010 in hoops. The hoop-skirt fad, however, proved short-lived, virtually ceasing with the advent of the Civil War in 1861. To make up for the declining market, Dunbar and Barnes turned to making springs for muskets and powder horns.

As the war went on to the south, drawing some of their workers into service with the Union Army, the partners also enlarged their clock-spring business and added springs that they sold to manufacturers of toys, sash balances, looms and other products. It is likely that political differences entered the picture around this time: Barnes was an ardent abolitionist and Republican, Dunbar a Southern sympathizer, or "Copperhead." At any rate, in 1863 the partnership was dissolved, Barnes assuming liabilities of $31,000 and paying Dunbar $11,000. Dunbar resumed spring-making on his own. Six decades later the business he built would once again come together with the Barnes family when the Associated Spring Corporation bought it in 1923.

For his part, Wallace Barnes also continued in springs. To reduce his dependence on imported English steel, he developed and patented an improved method of tempering and bought new machinery that would enable him to draw his own flat steel from round wire made in the United States. On May 29, 1866, however, before he could he could get the machinery into operation, the original wooden factory went up in a spectacular blaze, destroying almost everything.

Undeterred, Barnes moved a large barn from his farm on the west side of town and set it on the blackened foundations. It was used for manufacturing until replaced in 1917 by a new masonry structure, which served first as a factory and then as the company's administration building until Barnes Group moved into its modern headquarters in 1979 (the 1917 structure, modernized more recently as a rental office building, still houses management functions of the Associated Spring Group).

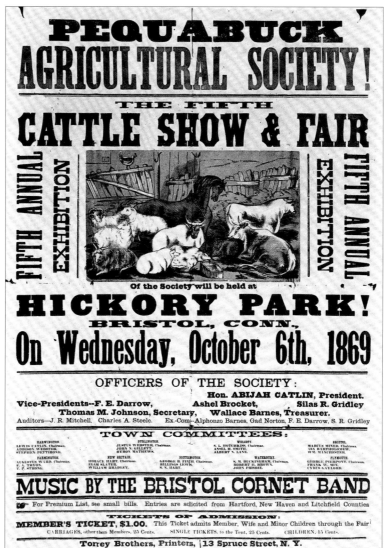

A handbill for Bristol's fair, with splendid type, listed Wallace Barnes as Treasurer, his father Alphonso as a member of the Executive Committee.

Wallace, (center) coon hunter extraordinary, poses with friends, a favorite hunting dog and paraphernalia of their sport.

From 1866 on, the Barnes spring business remained relatively small, at least compared to the hoop-skirt years. In 1874, Wallace employed 35 hands; he still depended mainly on water power from a sluice routed past the factory, using a small steam engine in seasons when the stream flow was down. Among his products were lamp springs for the Hitchcock Lamp Co. of Waterbury, level springs for Stanley Rule and Level of New Britain, clock springs for the Hamilton Clock Co. of Hamilton, Ontario, and other springs that were incorporated in doors, windows, burglar alarms, knitting machines, carriages and harness snaps.

In 1880, Wallace and his sons Carlyle and Harry, along with Irenus Atkins, organized the Barnes Brothers Clock Company to take over the old Atkins firm. The business did not prosper, however, as we shall see in the following chapter.

A GENIUS FOR MANUFACTURING

The era into which the Barnes Company was born saw Connecticut explode from a small agricultural state into an industrial giant that could—and did—make everything under the sun, selling much of it through itinerant Yankee peddlers who traveled from town to town (drawing below). In his book Yankee Dreamers and Doers, *Ellsworth Strong Grant* writes:

"Certainly, Connecticut can claim credit for the origin of more basic inventions and more important industries than any other state. Even before the Civil War it produced an astounding diversity of useful products that eased the average man's life.

"By that time Americans everywhere, thanks to the peripatetic peddler and the iron horse, could wake up in the morning to the striking of brass clocks made in Bristol, Thomaston, New Haven or Waterbury. They stepped on carpets woven in Thompsonville; softened their beards with Williams shaving soap from Glastonbury; put on clothes made from Somersville wool, Rockville cassimere, Norwich cotton or Manchester silk, fastened with Waterbury buttons, hooks and eyes, and sewed with Willimantic thread—including a New Haven shirt, a Bridgeport corset, a Meriden or Bristol hoop skirt, and cotton hose and suspenders from Middletown; dined on silverware from Meriden or tinware from Berlin, using a Parker coffee mill to grind the beans for their brew; sat in Hitchcock chairs; celebrated with a swig of Enfield cider brandy; smoked a cigar with a Windsor wrapper; cleaned their teeth with Comstock ivory toothpicks; put on a Danbury hat and a Naugatuck pair of rubbers; turned the key in a Blake or Yale lock....sailed in Mystic-built ships; hunted with a Colt revolver or Sharps rifle, using Hazardville powder....

"With the help of Howe's common pins housewives made new clothes on the Wilson sewing machine; their children looked up words in Noah Webster's Dictionary, printed in Hartford, under a Waterbury kerosene or whale oil brass lamp lit with a Beecher friction match....

"Gardens were planted with seeds packaged by Enfield Shakers and fields tilled with a Wethersfield plow or Higganum hoe; canning was done with Lyman's patented, air-tight fruit jars; sheep were sheared or butchered with Hotchkissville blades; mice were disposed of by a Bostwick mouse trap from Sharon; while fathers fished with Jenkins's spring-steel fish-hooks, blasted with Ensign-Bickford's safety fuse and cleared the forest with a Collinsville axe or machete."

And what accounted for this incredible burst of industrial pioneering? Grant attributes much of it to "the boundless energy, amazing skill, outright genius and motivation to succeed of the entrepreneurs themselves, who seized opportunity when it appeared, who never gave in to disappointment or disaster, who always sought new, better, cheaper ways of making more things for more people."

"For them," he concluded, "the race to fortune belonged only to the swift of foot, the stout of heart, the sharp of mind. Lesser mortals did not deserve to survive, at least as businessmen."

Excerpted, with permission, from *Yankee Dreamers and Doers*, Pequot Press, 1973.

From a wagonful of wares, a traveling Yankee peddler selects a Bristol-made clock to show his rapt audience.

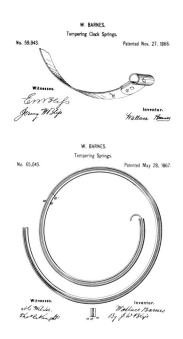

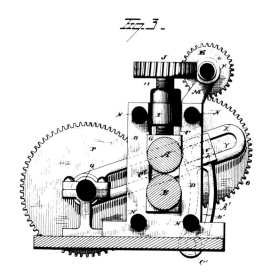

Ideas and action were Wallace Barnes's strong suits; finances and administration were not. Nevertheless, business reverses seldom got him down. A born optimist, with a ready smile that made him popular with fellow townsmen, he seemed not so much interested in money as he was in the challenge of something new. Above all, as he had amply demonstrated with his original investment of hoop-skirt wire, he was a old-fashioned Yankee trader at heart. Typical was an advertisement he placed in the local newspaper some years later, offering a family sewing machine for sale with the free-wheeling note: "Will trade for anything under the sun."

In fact, among his contemporaries—not only in Bristol but in agricultural circles across the nation—Barnes was known less as a manufacturer than as a leading trader of choice Jersey cattle, which American farmers had started to bring over from England in 1850 in attempts to improve their dairy herds.

Like other businessmen of the day who owned land, Wallace kept his hand in farming, tending extensive fruit orchards and buying his first Jersey stock the same year he went into the spring business on his own. At one point, records show that he owned 19 bulls and 38 cows, a sign that he kept his animals more for trading than the milk they could produce. The *Bristol Press* frequently carried reports that "Wallace Barnes sent 11 head of Jerseys to the auction sale in

New York," "Wallace Barnes sold his cow 'Daisy Girl' for $700" or "Wallace Barnes went to New York last week to attend the sale of Jersey stock [and] purchased a cow for $800." When he sold one of his prize Jersey bulls or heifers to a local farmer, he often took a number of the farmer's lesser stock in exchange.

In 1886, Barnes combined his growing knowledge of livestock with his early experience in drugs, developing a new medicine to combat the high rate of sterility and premature abortions that afflicted inbred Jersey stock. He was soon receiving orders from all over the country, and even shipped his medicine to customers as far away as Japan. In the years that his manufacturing business was faltering, it is likely that he made more money from cattle medicine than he did from springs.

As part of his interest in farming, Barnes enthusiastically helped to organize, and preside over, the Pequabuck Agricultural Society's annual cattle show and fair. Held each fall in Hickory Park—which was carved out of his own considerable farm property on the west side of town—it was enlarged to become the Bristol Fair, a gala event with midway amusements, snake charmers, fortune tellers, balloon ascensions and comely dancers whose modest garb was considered quite daring in the Victorian age. The fair's most popular event was the amateur horse race, in which prominent citizens rode their own mounts to the cheers of onlookers, and almost everyone, down to the most pious church deacon, delighted in making illegal bets.

Besides enjoying his prize livestock and fairs, Wallace sold pieces of his farm to other Bristolites looking for building lots, and was soon buying and selling properties in other sections of the growing town. Excited by this new form of trading, he extended his range to speculation along the Connecticut shore at Savin Rock, a local pleasure ground in West Haven, then to Martha's Vineyard Island off the Massachusetts coast, which in the 1870s was experiencing a real estate boom.

Starting on the island as a purchaser of a single lot, Barnes wound up buying out other investors in a major development and advertising lots for sale himself. To bolster his summer business, he erected a grand Victorian hotel named Oklahoma Hall on a scenic promontory overlooking the harbor, and even bought a 40-foot steam launch to carry his guests between the hotel and the nearby settlements of Vineyard Haven and Oak Bluffs.

Summers on the Vineyard were happy ones for Barnes, who loved the deep-sea fishing, the clambakes and the evening concerts and plays that he frequently staged at his hotel. Nevertheless, as it had before, the financial side of his business had gotten out of hand. He was unable to turn it around, and a year after his death the failing venture was finally sold by his sons. Not long after the hotel and its cottages were wiped out in a raging fire.

Wallace Barnes's zest for living included recreational pursuits closer to home. His favorite sport was coon-hunting, for which he invited friends—often his factory hands—on expeditions into the hills around Bristol, or into nearby New York State; after a successful outing he would return with as many as 40 raccoons, whose skins could be seen hanging outside his shed. He bought two or three good hunting dogs every year, generally from Kentucky, paying $200 or more for each. When the season was over, he often traded his surplus dogs to local farmers, taking some of their livestock in exchange. He always kept one special favorite as a house dog, which faithfully followed him wherever he went.

Another interest was music, which Barnes enjoyed from an early age, joining the Bristol Brass Band when he was 15 years old. Wallace was one of four "cornucopatists," or cornet players, in the band, which gave concerts on the town green and often took part in parades and political rallies in Bristol, Hartford, Litchfield and other towns. Later in his life he donated a much-needed piano for use in performances at the town hall (his old Crinoline Hall, which he had sold to the city fathers). After one concert in 1884, a well-attended affair that he managed and promoted himself, the *Bristol Press* reported: "Mr. Hilliard of New York with his splen-

did tenor voice met the expectations of the audience. Mrs. Rockwood of Montreal did not seem to be in as good voice as usual. Local talent included C. F. Barnes, flutist and celloist."

"C.F." was Wallace's son Carlyle, who was a more serious musician than his father, and who was also to run the family business with sounder results.

In the mid-1880s, Wallace was instrumental in building a new theater on Main Street called the Odeon, where the Bristol Trio Club and Orchestra, which included C.F. as cello soloist, had their practice rooms upstairs. The Odeon was the scene of many popular musicals and plays, to which an admission of 15 cents was charged—until the wooden structure, like so many others, went up in flames in 1888. Though Wallace, as a Bristol fire commissioner, had seen to it that the town owned two steam-powered pumpers, fires had to be kindled in their boilers after alarms were sounded. By the time water could be sprayed on the Odeon blaze, it was too late.

When Wallace Barnes died on March 28, 1893, at the age of 65, his holdings were appraised at $67,905, including $40,860 in real estate, not exactly a pauper's lot but one that included little in liquid assets that were needed by his business at a critical time.

To his family and friends, however—and to later generations of employees— he left a greater legacy: the colorful memory of Yankee trader, and a human being, that is remembered still.

The Barnes factory in 1882, with its work force seen in front.

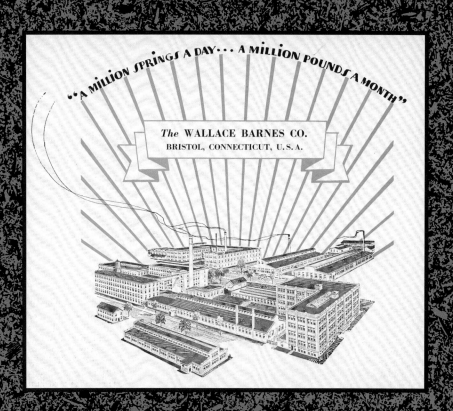

"A MILLION SPRINGS A DAY ... A MILLION POUNDS A MONTH"

The WALLACE BARNES CO.
BRISTOL, CONNECTICUT, U.S.A.

CHAPTER TWO

SPRINGS FOR EVERYONE

An early Barnes advertisement, with a view of the company's plants.

Any Spring; Any Material; Any Quantity

— COMPANY ADVERTISEMENT

But for his elder son, the company that Wallace Barnes started might well have joined many other 19th Century enterprises that foundered and sank without a trace. Though a reluctant industrialist in the beginning, Carlyle Fuller Barnes shouldered family responsibility when he had to, brought the business back from the brink of bankruptcy and guided it into profitable new fields. He often remarked that he wanted Barnes to become the "Tiffany of the spring business." He largely succeeded in his goal.

Carlyle and Lena Barnes enjoying a musical interlude.

The oldest of five children, Carlyle inherited not only his middle name from his mother but much of her common sense as well. Described as "a woman of exceptional character," Eliza Jane Fuller was a descendant of Edward Fuller, who arrived in New England on the *Mayflower*, and the daughter of Thomas Fuller, a successful Bristol clockmaker, who passed on to her an unusual degree of business acuity for a woman of those days. In turn, she tried to see to it that her son did not scatter his energies among many interests, as her husband Wallace was prone to do, but instead urged him to concentrate on one job and do it well. In a very real way, the company owes its continued existence to a mother's concern.

For a considerable period, however, there was doubt that Carlyle would be a businessman at all. From the precocious age of two, he exhibited a fascination with music, a love that would continue through his life. To expose him to more practical disciplines, his parents took him out of grade school in Bristol and sent him to a small private school in Hartford, the Pavilion Family School, where, to their relief, the headmaster reported that the youngster "maintained a high standing in scholarship, as well as a good name for sobriety and orderly behavior." To complete his secondary education, Carlyle was packed off to Williston Academy in Easthampton, Massachusetts, one of the first of its kind to place scientific courses on an equal plane with the classics.

After graduating from Williston in 1870, Carlyle returned to Hartford to gain some working experience. For three years he was employed in a firm that supplied steel to Barnes and other spring makers, then spent four years as an accountant for Cheney Brothers, a major manufacturer of silk. Though he did reasonably well at his tasks, Carlyle was torn: deep down, he still wanted to be a musician. And so, in January of 1877, at the age of 24, he set sail from New York aboard the North German Lloyd steamer *Bremen*, determined to give it a try.

In Munich, young Barnes studied under some of Europe's finest musicians, specializing in the flute. He also had a chance to sample Old World culture, visiting art galleries and historic attractions as far south as Rome. During his three years on the Continent, however, he evidently began to realize his limitations as a professional musician, especially in view of the time and dedication that would be required to reach the top. At this point his father wrote him of plans to reorganize the Atkins Clock Company, offering him and his younger brother Harry a chance to run the new enterprise.

Carlyle decided to come home. At

Carlyle Barnes in later years.

his father's suggestion, he stopped over in England to meet officials of the Sheffield and Birmingham mills that were the company's principal suppliers of steel, a detour that would prove of later value in keeping the business alive.

Whether it was due to lack of capital, unfamiliarity with new technical demands or competition from larger clock makers, the Barnes Brothers Clock Company lasted only four years. As an added problem, the brothers had to cope with their father's cheerful habit of taking money from one of his businesses to pay another's debts (after Wallace's repeated borrowing from the company to trade in his favorite Jersey cattle, Carlyle confided to a friend that he had grown to hate the sight of a cow). It probably did not help

The Wallace Barnes Company poses for a group portrait in 1895, two years after its founder's death. Wallace's brother Thomas is the bearded gentleman at far left in the first row; his son Carlyle ("C.F.") is at far right in the second row; C.F.'s cousin Jack is fifth from right in the back. The ladies, from left, are Catherine and Elizabeth Hackett, Edith and Sarah Fosberg and Nellie Lambert.

that widespread political unrest around the country, in the form of the Populist Party and other movements, was beginning to affect business as a whole. In any case, the Barnes brothers gave up clocks and went back to making springs.

While not poring over his ledgers, the elder son found time to continue his musical bent. He assumed the leadership of the Bristol Cornet Band, which had earned a reputation as one of the best in the state, and also led the Bristol Orchestra, soloing on the cello in addition to the flute. Bristol's Odeon theater, which his father had helped to start, became the scene of spirited concerts and operettas like *The Mikado* and *H.M.S. Pinafore*.

During rehearsals and performances, Carlyle gradually became aware of a new interest: a young lady named Lena Forbes, who had graduated from the Cincinnati College of Music and was

supporting herself in Bristol by giving private piano lessons. They were married on October 8, 1885. Fellow members of the Bristol Orchestra contributed a chinaware service to send them on their way as newlyweds.

The turning point in the life of Carlyle Barnes, and the company, came when his father died in 1893. Despite the brothers' efforts, the family's business affairs were still in disarray, with substantial obligations and little cash. The demand for clock springs, the firm's basic product, had been steadily decreasing as more and more clock companies turned to making their own; springs for mechanical toys and other uses, which the company added to make up the deficit, were not enough to hold the line. Moreover, the nation was entering the depths of another "panic," a depression that would last for four dismal years.

Business sages of the community advised "C. F.," as he was now widely known, to get out of springs for good, but he decided to put all his eggs in one basket instead. He persuaded the firm's suppliers in England, who remembered him kindly from his earlier visit, to extend him additional credit for steel. He drew on a close friendship with William Ingraham of the Ingraham clock company, which had become Bristol's largest industry, to secure several personal loans. He worked long hours at the factory handling accounts, often pitching in on the production line himself. It was fortunate that he and his wife had a modest outside income from their music. They needed every penny of it.

To bolster its dwindling capital, in 1897 the family business was incorporated as the Wallace Barnes Company and 300 shares of stock were issued at $100 a share. Carlyle's brother-in-law, W. C. Ladd, was elected president (he was later succeeded by Carlyle's mother, Eliza, who held the office until her death in 1903). Serving in the key roles of secretary and treasurer was C. F. himself.

At this point, while the firm was still struggling, a new market opened up unexpectedly, much as it had for the infant company four decades before. This time it was not hoop skirts, but bicycles. "Wheels," as they were called, had been around since the 1860s but had seen limited use, mainly because they were ungainly "high-wheelers" whose tires were made of hard rubber and steel. Then, with the development of low two-wheelers, and the invention of the pneumatic tire in the 1890s by an Irishman named James Dunlop, almost overnight bicycles became a popular means of transportation in Europe and the United States.

The Barnes Company, as it had before, moved quickly to cash in on the fad, turning out thousands of springs for bicycle bells. The factory also made other items like toe springs, which held cyclists' feet firmly on the pedals. The biggest sellers by far, however, were trouser guards—simple leg clips that Barnes churned out by the millions, help-

Starting in the 1890s, bicycles provided a booming market for Barnes-made springs. The earliest models to be seen in Bristol were high-wheelers like this Columbia, shown with its proud owner George Moulthrope, a Dunbar employee, who bought it with $200 he won in a lottery. The 4-foot wheel, with ungeared pedals and hard rubber rims, made every trip a precarious adventure. Cycling caught on only after the development of the "safety bicycle," which had two smaller wheels, a chain drive, softer pneumatic tires and a more affordable price tag.

BRISTOL'S AUTO PIONEERS

Though better known for its clocks and springs, Bristol for a while pioneered in the making of automobiles, a fact that helped lay the groundwork for Barnes's leadership in supplying valve springs and other parts to the automotive field.

As early as 1873 Rufus Porter, a local resident and the first editor of Scientific American magazine, constructed a horseless carriage that he claimed could reach 50 miles per hour. Porter formed the Steam Carriage Company to produce his invention for sale, but the experiment failed when it was found that his vehicle could not stand up under the vibration of the steam engine it employed.

Another enthusiast was Frederick N. Manross of Bristol's F. N. Manross & Sons, makers of hair springs, shown here with his wife Sylvia posing in early "His" and "Her" models outside their garage. His magnificent Winton convertible, which he bought in

Cleveland in 1898, was the first gasoline-powered car to operate in Connecticut; the next year he purchased the daintier three-wheeled Knox for Sylvia, who became the first woman driver in the state. In 1902, Manross orga-

nized the Bristol Car Company to make his own automobiles, a successful enterprise that was eventually absorbed by the Corbin Motor Car Co. of nearby New Britain. (The Manross spring business was acquired in 1937 by

Associated Spring.)

Other Bristol manufacturers tried their hand at the horseless carriage trade. New Departure—which under the eye of Albert Rockwell had grown into a sizeable company making bicycle bells and coaster brakes —produced the 85-horsepower Haupt-Rockwell convertible touring car, one of the finest automobiles of the era and the first to use an engine cast in a single block. Rockwell also established the Bristol Engineering Company to build taxicabs, the first of the familiar "Yellow Cabs" used around the United States. His weakness was not technology, but an apparently reckless desire for expansion without regard to financial consequences. The result was that in 1913 Rockwell was replaced by his brother-in-law, Dewitt Page, who went on to build New Departure into a leading maker of ball bearings, and to amass one of Connecticut's largest fortunes for himself.

ing countless gentlemen and schoolboys from getting their baggy cuffs caught in sprockets or wheels.

The bicycle boom led to a long-overdue modernization of the firm's production lines, which were supervised by Carlyle's younger cousin Jack, a self-taught expert in the details of spring-making and a popular leader on the factory floor. A Fitchburg steam engine was installed to take over power requirements from the plant's ancient water wheel. A

new tempering furnace, fired by coal, was introduced to reduce the need for huge sheds full of cordwood, which had to be cut and hauled in laboriously each year from the neighboring hills.

In 1897 the company purchased its first piece of automated machinery, mainly to keep up with the demand for trouser guards. Before long, front-office clerks were marveling at their own shiny new labor-saving device: the firm's first adding machine. By now the prospering company was employing some 70 people, compared with 20 or 30 when Carlyle took over from his father a half-dozen years before.

Meanwhile, the boom in bicycles was leading to an even more sweeping revolution in transportation: the motor car. Around 1900, springs destined for use in automobiles began to appear in the company's books. At first the orders were small, and since the earliest models were assembled largely by enterprising mechanics in New England—most of them within a hundred miles of Bristol, and a few within the city limits (see box)—the manufacturers often drove to the plant to pick up deliveries themselves.

But as the industry grew, so did the need for thousands of valve springs, clutch springs, suspension springs, starter springs and a hundred other items with-

out which automobiles could not run. The "horseless carriage" would come to dominate the spring business, particularly when Henry Ford began mass-producing his famous Model Ts and the center of the booming industry shifted to the Midwest.

In an era that witnessed an incredible host of new inventions, automobiles were not the only gadgets that depended on springs. More and more Americans were learning to use typewriters, cash registers, telephones, ice-cream makers and sewing machines. Springs were needed for incandescent lamps, electric motors, centrifugal pumps. Pullman sleeping cars had to have big springs to cushion the ride on steel rails, and smaller ones to counterbalance their pull-down upper berths. To while away leisure

The Bristol Cornet Band, which Carlyle served as leader and soloist.

hours, people everywhere were buying pianos, player pianos, small household organs and a new marvel called the phonograph or "talking machine."

Barnes made its share of springs for many of these products, including thousands of wind-up springs it helped develop for the the Victor Talking Machine Company's "Victrola." But good springs could be made only from uniformly high-quality steel, which in the absence of reliable American suppliers still had to be imported. Ever since Wallace Barnes had seen his first attempts thwarted by the disastrous fire of 1866, company officials had longed for a steel mill of their own.

In 1908, Carlyle Barnes bought land in the Forestville section east of Bristol, convenient to the railroad line, with just such a plan in mind. Work on a railroad siding was begun in 1914; the mill itself, under the eye of superintendent Lyman Adams, finally went into operation in the fall of 1915. It would soon be turning out cold-rolled spring steel that was the equal of any in the world.

Even before the new mill had been started, another generation of Barneses was coming on the scene. Carlyle and Lena Barnes were the proud parents of two sons, Fuller, born in 1887, and his brother Harry, who joined the family two years later in 1889.

Fuller Forbes Barnes, who would lead the company through its next wave of expansion, grew up like many boys in the 1890s, though a serious hip injury curbed normal athletics for awhile. By the time he was 13 he had recovered and was earning enough money, mowing lawns and selling dandelion greens, to buy his own bicycle. Though his parents were not yet wealthy—for a time they rented the second floor of their home to make ends meet—they often took the boys on family outings. These included some memorable rides in the new Stanley Steamer Carlyle had bought, a gleaming but often cranky automobile that had neither top nor windshield, and whose boiler had to be filled with water every few miles in the course of a trip.

After three years at Bristol High School, where Fuller managed average grades, the family's finances had improved enough to send him off for another two years to Phillips Academy in Andover, Massachusetts, from which, somewhat to his parents' astonishment, he graduated with a prize for scholarship. Like many of his Andover classmates, he went on to Yale, where he took liberal arts courses, sampled fraternity life and sang in the glee club and chapel choir. On graduating in 1910, he joined several classmates on a summer tour of Europe, then, dutifully returning to Bristol, began work in the family company, which at the time had somewhat over 200 employees.

Harry Clarke Barnes, meanwhile, like his older brother had attended Bristol's Federal Hill School, near the family's home, then had gone on to Holbrook Military Academy, where his lifetime love of baseball started with his position as first baseman on the school team. Though it was assumed that Harry would go into the company, too, he at first followed in his father's footsteps, studying at the New England Conservatory of Music in Boston, then pursuing his music for a year in Munich before joining the family business in 1913 at age 24.

During their training programs at the company, young Fuller and Harry learned techniques from skilled mechanics, assisted in making spiral and flat springs, worked in the front office figuring estimates and costs. By the time Fuller had finished his apprenticeship his father, Carlyle, whose health had been failing, thought well enough of his elder son's abilities to pass on some of the burden to him.

In 1913, Fuller Forbes Barnes was made general manager and treasurer of the Wallace Barnes Company. He celebrated by marrying another member of an old Bristol family, Myrtle Aurelia Ives. All things considered, it was a big year for a man who had just turned 26.

The next year, however, was to prove an even bigger one in the life of the company and its new general manager. A shot fired in the streets of an obscure town named Sarajevo signaled the beginning of World War I.

As quickly as it could, the Barnes factory turned to the war orders that started pouring in, most of them for unfamiliar products that required extremely close tolerances and, at the same time,

high production speed. Moreover, many of the first orders came from foreign governments, creating considerable confusion. While those in English were hard enough to fill, blueprints from Russia, with instructions in the Cyrillic alphabet, required even greater ingenuity.

Many of the foreign contracts were for small fuse springs and primer parts, and the company was so short of help

that it let employees take the work home. In their living rooms or kitchens, Barnes men and women placed individual springs on cards and packed them in boxes of 1,000, at 35 cents a thousand, an average worker packing 4,000 or 5,000 a night. On many an evening Fuller Barnes brought a load back from the factory and he and his wife, Myrtle, spent several hours doing their share.

Soldiers and sailors, including hometown boys, march down Main Street in Bristol during World War I. Among cheering bystanders are many in fashionable straw "boater" hats.

THE INDISPENSABLE SPRING

Though most springs are hidden from view, few things would work without them in our world. Billions of springs go into everything we use, from ordinary ball-point pens to sophisticated satellites in space. The spring-making divisions of Barnes Group manufacture thousands of different types, ranging in size from tiny hair springs used in instruments to massive coils that reduce vibration in heavy industrial machines.

A spring is essentially any device, usually made of tempered steel, that absorbs, stores and releases mechanical energy, returning to its original position when an outside force is removed.

Compression springs, like those used in coil-type shock absorbers and automobile engine valves, are used to cushion pressing forces. Extension springs—a simple example is an old-fashioned screen-door closer—stretch when pulled and contract to their original shape when released. Torsion springs, like the mainsprings of mechanical clocks and wind-up toys, work by a twisting or unwinding motion. Flat springs, in the form of clips, washers and leaf springs, are formed into many shapes to absorb pressure, or to create pressure to hold parts together.

At home, springs go into the beds we sleep on, the alarm clock or clock radio that wakes us up, the switches that turn the lights on, the thermostats and furnace burners that keep us warm, the windows that we open and close. In the bathroom, faucets, toilets, electric shavers, aerosol cans and pump dispensers depend on springs, as does almost everything in the kitchen: refrigerator, mixer, coffeemaker, toaster, range, dishwasher, waste disposer,

Products of Associated Spring

kitchen cabinets and more.

On our way out to work or shopping, small springs catch and lock the front door; large ones make it easier to open the garage. The car we drive incorporates hundreds of different kinds of springs—without them the ignition wouldn't go on, the engine wouldn't turn over and the pedals, doors, windows, horn and dashboard instruments wouldn't work. At the office, elevators, computers, typewriters, calculators and other equipment depend on springs. Back home at the end of the day, springs help operate our air conditioners, TV sets, telephones, answering machines, cameras, musical instruments, sporting equipment, bicycles, lawnmowers, power tools and children's toys.

Not all springs are hidden. Two of the most evident, and indispensable, inventions that we use daily are simple torsion springs: the paper clip and the safety pin. The latter, in fact, traces its origins to one of the first known uses of springs—small clasps and brooches known as "fibulae," used by ancient peoples to hold their clothing in place.

Not all of the work was done by hand. During the early war years, three Barnes employees contributed a major technical advance to the history of springs. On January 4, 1916, Adolph B. L. Linberg, John Ernest Andrew and Henry C. Wright of Bristol were awarded a U.S. patent, which they assigned to their employer, on an automatic spring-making machine that could turn out either right- or left-hand torsion springs, and could also be adapted to produce compression or extension springs.

With the experience gained from the initial overseas orders, the company was better equipped when America itself entered the war in 1917. Since the U.S. armed forces were woefully short of up-to-date guns and ammunition, however, their needs were huge.

Especially acute was the demand for machine guns, whose value the German Army had foreseen—and was using with devastating effect. The pressure to make up the deficit fell largely on Connecticut gunsmiths like Winchester, Marlin-Rockwell and Colt, which for vital springs and other components turned to

Barnes. The leading model, the 30-caliber Browning, of which more than 50,000 were manufactured in Connecticut, incorporated no less than 14 parts from Barnes production lines. The company's rolling mill also produced almost all of the carbon spring steel used for links that joined individual machine-gun bullets into ammunition belts. In addition, Barnes springs went into disposable magazine clips for Browning automatic rifles, the famous "BARs."

One measure of Barnes's war effort was the number of springs it churned out for Uncle Sam—an estimated 90 million. Another was the size of its payroll. When hostilities broke out in the early summer of 1914, less than 300 workers were employed. By the time the Armistice was signed in the fall of 1918, that number had almost quintupled to 1,400. People were working in the old factory buildings; in the rolling mill; in the new five-story headquarters the company erected in 1917; and in the machine shop of the Garrigus Company, which Barnes had bought and renamed the Bristol Machine Tool Company. Here workers made grinders and milling machines, both for Barnes's own production lines and for other firms that manufactured small arms for the military.

With the end of the war, much of the special machinery had to be scrapped, and the company was forced to adjust to peacetime realities with a smaller labor force. But a new, and even greater, era of expansion lay just ahead.

A whimsical calendar reminded customers of the virtues of Barnes-made springs.

CHAPTER THREE

BOOM, BUST AND GLOBAL WAR

*A 1928 advertisement traces the company's adaptations
to changing markets: hoop skirts, muskets, buggies, typewriters and bicycles,
motor cars, appliances, machine guns, airplanes and radios.*

It ain't the individual nor the army as a whole
But the everlastin' team work of every bloomin' soul.

— RUDYARD KIPLING, QUOTED IN *THE MAIN SPRING,* 1919

A rousing call for employee involvement appears on an early cover of the company magazine, which was edited by Fuller F. Barnes.

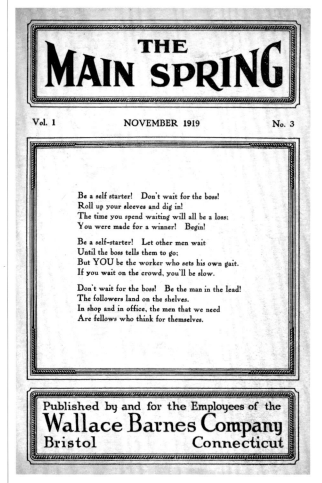

The "Roaring Twenties" would witness the most spectacular boom in the nation's history, followed by the most spectacular bust—and, within a few years, the world's most devastating war. They would also see the Wallace Barnes Company, and spring-making, come of age.

At first, the period following World War I was a curious mixture of relief, recession and reform. The 1920s opened with two new Constitutional amendments going into effect—one giving women the right to vote, the other prohibiting everyone's right to buy a drink. Just as people were trying to adjust to these major developments, an economic downturn shook business once more, among other things leading Barnes's struggling machine-tool operation to shut its doors.

Nevertheless, demands pent up by the war years soon set the economy afire. Consumer goods of every description poured out of U.S. factories, credit was easy, and Americans discovered the pleasures of jazz, the movies and bathtub gin. People happily went into debt to buy new-fangled luxuries that included vacuum cleaners, refrigerators and ever shinier automobiles, the "Tin Lizzies" that were beginning to change the very structure of

The Main Spring *specialized in chatty accounts of employee doings. A 1920 issue included this snapshot, captioned: "No, these are not Mexican bandits, but our President, C.F. Barnes, and party somewhere en route to San Diego."*

the American economy and way of life.

Besides making vital parts for the automotive market, including valve springs, clutch springs and springs for the newly invented Bendix automatic starter, Barnes found new clients in other fields. With the first public radio broadcast—from KDKA, Pittsburgh, announcing the returns of the 1920 Harding-Cox Presidential election—came demands for springs in broadcasting and receiving equipment, including millions of household radios. The motion picture industry, just hitting its stride, needed springs for cameras and projectors, and would require even more sophisticated equipment after the introduction of "talkies" in 1927. Still more springs went into typewriters, washing machines, electrical switches and motors, clocks and watches, children's wind-up toys. With the rise of bootlegging and big-time gangsters, Barnes even filled—and tested at pointblank range—at least one order for spring steel to be used in bulletproof vests.

The era's many technical advances, in turn, led to greater emphasis on precision manufacturing and research, particularly in the science of metallurgy, which was aimed at developing better steel that got "tired" less easily after constant use. This property, called fatigue value, had to be carefully controlled to avoid not only costly equipment breakdowns but possible injuries from defective products. Out of the new research, which some called the "engineering approach," would come stronger springs of steel and other alloys

OLD-STYLE COMPANY PICNIC

At 11 a.m. on Saturday, September 6, 1919, the Barnes factory whistle blew, signaling employees to go home and get dressed in their picnic best. More than 600 merrymakers soon assembled and, to the strains of a 30-piece band, boarded trolley cars and automobiles for the procession to Bristol's Lake Compounce amusement park.

The Wallace Barnes Company's Second Annual Picnic and Barbecue—a "grand and glorious outing"—was reported in detail in the first issue of The Main Spring, the company's monthly magazine. The festivities started with a prodigious midday meal: "All sat down to one of [Compounce's] justly famed sheep barbecues, and what a delicious dinner it was. Heaping plates of tender lamb and corn, and pota-

The Barnes tug-of-war team, which beat Ingraham in two straight pulls.

toes and lots of other things that tasted so good, disappeared like magic before the attack of the hungry crowd."

After lunch and a group picture at the baseball field, everyone gathered for the big game between the Factory and the Barnes "Get-To-Gether Club." Factory scored first, but with the help of strong pitching and a homer from Teddy Zanhke, Get-To-Gether emerged triumphant, 8 to 4, much to the joy of its wildly rooting fans.

The afternoon rolled along merrily with a girl's ball-throwing contest, in which Edith Gutska won first place and a $2.50 gold piece. In the foot races, Earle Sparks took the men's 100-yard dash. Helen Rogaski, who had wisely changed to bloomers, romped home in the women's

dash. Antoinette Guertin was first over the line balancing a potato on her spoon; teamed with Victoria Glynn, she also won the live chicken chase, taking the prize home for Sunday dinner. After the swimming race, also captured by Sparks, all gathered in the lakeside dance pavilion, where, amid general dancing to fox trots and one steps, Miss Gutska and Ed Dalger edged out Miss Guertin and Charlie Unkleback in order to claim the coveted waltzing prize.

"Six-thirty and cars for home came all too soon," The Main Spring noted, "but everyone, tired and happy, left Compounce with the thought that the 1919 picnic was the best ever."

Determined to go themselves one better, the following year Barnes employees invited their

counterparts from the E. Ingraham Company, Bristol's famous clockmaker, to join the fun and games. In the ensuing competitions, it was reported, Barnes athletes won eight first places to Ingraham's four, including the all-important tug of war and the relay race around the lake (photos).

The 1,200 attendees were then entertained by the Barnes minstrel chorus, cornet band and barbershop quartet. The climax came with solos from Ralph Joerres, captain of the winning relay team, who rendered "The Love Nest" in a stirring baritone, and Mary Canfield, who captivated the audience with a number called "Cuddle Up."

If you don't think that company picnic was a humdinger, the last trolley back to Bristol left at 9:30 p.m.

Helen Rogaski, chief point-getter.

The Barnes relay team

that could be relied on to perform specific jobs more safely and efficiently than springs ever had before.

To handle an increasing volume of business—now approaching $2 million a year in sales—the company contemplated expansion again, this time with broader horizons in mind. The initial move, in 1921, was to lease a small plant in Hamilton, Ontario, and set up a subsidiary, Wallace Barnes Co., Ltd., to gain a toehold in Canada's thriving industrial belt.

Even more important to the future, it was becoming apparent, was the Midwestern United States, particularly Detroit, with its humming automobile factories, and Chicago, an industrial hub where Barnes had many customers as well. Since building new plants far from home, in competition with established spring makers, could prove an expensive and risky proposition, it was decided to explore a merger with one or more of them instead.

Among the candidates was the William D. Gibson Company, which had started life in a basement on Chicago's LaSalle Street in 1869 making upholstery springs for beds. Despite the great Chicago Fire of 1871, which destroyed its modest quarters—and another blaze in 1888, which nearly wiped out a larger plant—Gibson rebuilt its business to include springs for agricultural implements and machinery, adding saddle springs for bicycles and spring stays for the "Empress" skirts that be-

came fashionable in the 1890s.

A pioneer in spring design known for high quality, Gibson was becoming to the Midwest what the Barnes Company was to the East. Its exhibit at the Columbian Exposition of 1893 won the "highest award for excellence of material and workmanship." By 1894 the firm was making springs for farm equipment, washing machines, trolleys, organs and textile looms.

After a third fire gutted its factory in 1905 (one wonders how American industry survived at all), the company managed to recover once more. Its 1912 catalog listed 76 types of springs, including several used in the growing automobile industry. Gibson gradually concentrated on springs for tractors, automobiles and trucks, and later made valve and other springs for the famous "Liberty Engine" that powered airplanes in World War I.

Another candidate Barnes had its eye on was the Raymond Manufacturing Company of Corry, Pennsylvania, which also made springs for the automotive and aircraft industries. The firm had been founded by Murray Raymond in 1883 to manufacture a single, novel product he had invented—a "baby jumper," which consisted of a child-sized seat suspended from overhead by two coiled springs. Production started in a small room over a broom factory on North Center Street.

Raymond energetically promoted his new gadget in person by traveling around to expositions and fairs, winning a medal at the Cincinnati Industrial Exposi-

In the 1920s, a worker stands next to one of the largest springs ever produced at the Bristol plant. No one remembers exactly what it was made for, but a veteran employee recalls stories that a second-story window had to be removed in order to lower the monster to the ground.

In 1882 Murray Raymond, far right, invented a spring-suspended "baby jumper," demonstrated here by his young son Frank, and began producing it in the old Opera House building on Corry, Pennsylvania's North Center Street, below. Four decades later Frank would merge the company with Barnes and the Gibson Company of Chicago to form Associated Spring.

tion of 1884. At each site he rented a booth and installed a number of jumpers in which young children could bounce happily under his watchful eye, leaving their grateful mothers free to enjoy other exhibits and entertainments—and, of course, to buy one of his indispensable pacifiers when they came back.

As Raymond's business bounced along, and upward, he diversified into other lines, including hat-and-coat racks, broom holders and carpet-beating whips, as well as saddle springs for bicycles and anti-rattling coils for horse-drawn buggies. With the advent of the first airplanes, the firm started to make springs for aircraft engines, supplying orders to the Wright Brothers' factory in Dayton, Ohio, as early as 1910 and to the Curtiss Aeroplane and Motor Company of Buffalo, New York, in 1915. During the 1920s, company records note with pride that planes using Curtiss engines with Raymond valve springs set records for both speed (243 miles per hour) and continuous flight (420 hours in the air).

After talks with officials of the Gibson and Raymond firms, Fuller and Harry Barnes proposed that they explore the idea of a combined effort, centered on the establishment of a new, jointly owned plant to serve auto makers in Detroit. The first formal meeting was held at the Hotel Lafayette in Buffalo on September 7, 1922. Present were the Barnes brothers, Gibson's Warren Howe and Alexander Peterson and Raymond's Frank Raymond and Federal Whittlesey. Appointing themselves a "Committee of Six," these gentlemen agreed to authorize an independent appraisal of the three companies on which a merger could be based. They also appointed Harry Barnes, Peterson and Whittlesey as a subcommittee to look into available properties in and around Detroit.

An investigation by W. J. Black, Barnes's Detroit sales representative,

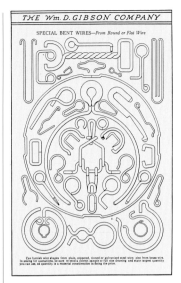

A page from Gibson's 1912 catalog displays an artistic composition of small, spring-like parts that the company could furnish on order.

The "Committee of Six" that formed Associated Spring in 1923. In front: Federal E. Whittlesey and Warren D. Howe. In back: Harry C. Barnes, Alexander B. Peterson, Frank M. Raymond, Fuller F. Barnes.

In 1923 the plants of the Associated Spring Corp. looked like this

WALLACE BARNES COMPANY

THE WM. D. GIBSON COMPANY

RAYMOND MANUFACTURING COMPANY

DUNBAR BROTHERS COMPANY

BARNES-GIBSON-RAYMOND

THE WALLACE BARNES CO., LTD.

WALLACE BARNES ROLLING MILL

SCREW MACHINE PLANT—WALLACE BARNES CO.

A composite portrait of the newly formed company.

When the bank agreed to sell the property for $100,000, the Committee of Six met in Detroit on November 1, completed the purchase and named the new venture Barnes-Gibson–Raymond, Inc.

With this first step behind them, the principals worked out the details of consolidating the three companies under the aegis of a holding company, which they christened the Associated Spring Corporation and incorporated under the laws of the State of New York on January 6, 1923. As officers of the new company, the directors elected Fuller Barnes, President; Frank Raymond, First Vice President; Harry Barnes, Secretary; Warren Howe, Treasurer; and Alexander Peterson, Assistant Treasurer.

In announcing the merger to the press, the new officers explained somewhat sweepingly that the association would "result in the greatly increased benefits to be derived from having five plants so arranged geographically as to cover practically the entire manufacturing field of the United States and Canada." Of special importance was the new Barnes-Gibson-Raymond plant, from which it would be possible to "serve the many users in and around Detroit, notably in the automobile field, who are large users of springs." To allay any apprehension, particularly among employees, the announcement stressed that the three companies would continue to operate as they had before, with "absolutely no change in either the management or the personnel of any of the organizations involved."

turned up several options, which were duly inspected by the subcommittee in mid-October. The most likely was the plant of the Zenith Foundry Company, which a mortgage foreclosure had placed in the hands of the Peninsula State Bank.

Two months later Barnes further strengthened the venture by buying out the Dunbar Brothers Company of Bristol, the descendant of the spring-making firm with which Wallace Barnes had collaborated in the days of the hoop-skirt craze. Meanwhile, key personnel from all the companies of Associated Spring were encouraged to visit each others' plants to share methods of management, engineering, purchasing, production, accounting and sales.

Nurtured by the Roaring Twenties, the infant corporation grew lustily. From 1923 to 1929, total sales increased a respectable 85 per cent, boosted mainly by growing demands from the automotive, appliance and aviation industries. During the same period the considerable sum of $4 million was invested in improving production facilities, including the new operation in Detroit. The company, which by now had decided to reincorporate in Delaware for tax purposes, also acquired a major share in one of its principal suppliers of steel wire, the Washburn Wire Company of Phillipsdale, Rhode Island. It also bought the Cook Spring Company of Ann Arbor, Michigan, which made springs for automobiles, adding it to the Barnes-Gibson-Raymond division.

In was during this period that one of spring-making's most important new technologies, shot-peening, came about—almost by chance—when engineers in BGR's Detroit plant were trying to improve the fatigue value of automobile springs. After forming and grinding

FULLER BARNES

To his contemporaries, Fuller Forbes Barnes was a man of wide-ranging visions—and the drive necessary to attain them. After joining the company on his graduation from Yale in 1910, he quickly rose to Treasurer and in 1913 added the title of General Manager, continuing in those roles until the death of his father Carlyle in 1926, when he was elected President. Three years earlier he had been the main force in putting Barnes together with two other family-owned companies to form Associated Spring. Over the next three decades he steered Associated through major expansions, the Great Depression and World War II, handing over the reins in 1953 to his son Carlyle F. ("Hap") Barnes.

Fuller Barnes, who had become a recognized leader in the industry, was the primary founder and first President of the Spring Manufacturers Association. He also served as an officer or director of many other organizations, including the Bristol Bank and Trust, Bristol Brass, Connecticut Light and Power and Southern New England Telephone. For awhile he tried his hand at politics, and was twice elected a State Senator from his district, in 1929 and 1931. Perhaps closest to his heart, however, was the Bristol Hospital, which he served as President and principal fund raiser for 30 years, helping it to erect a modern, well-equipped building in 1925.

An avid fisherman and

golfer, in his later years Fuller became absorbed in a new challenge, the making of needlepoint tapestries, creating large pieces on classical and Biblical themes and crafting the frames for them in his home woodworking shop.

He also helped to develop Bristol's American Clock and Watch Museum, a unique collection of period timepieces started by his friend Edward Ingraham to celebrate the region's clock-making history. One of its main galleries, displaying a series of priceless grandfather clocks, is housed in a wing donated by Fuller Barnes. Named after his ancestor Ebenezer Barnes, it incorporates the original paneling and ceilings from Ebenezer's house, which was built in 1728 as Bristol's first permanent home.

the springs, it was customary to wire-brush them to remove all traces of grinding abrasive. In an effort to speed up this time-consuming operation, one version of the story goes, someone put a test lot of springs into a sand-blasting machine containing steel grit.

Another, more interesting, version is that several barrels of springs had been left on an open loading dock, where a rainstorm had caused them to rust. Not wanting the order rejected, Chief Engineer Franz Zimmerli ordered them cleaned up in the sand-blaster. When the customer rejected the batch anyway because they had a rough, dull surface, Zimmerli took the springs back and ran a series of tests on them in the fatigue laboratory he had just set up. Much to everyone's surprise, the springs had a much

HARRY BARNES

"**Kind**," "*gentle*," "*a warm human being*"—*they were words that people often used about Harry Clarke Barnes. Almost everyone liked him, from directors in the board room to workers on the production line.*

Born in Bristol in 1889, the second son of Carlyle F. Barnes, Harry at first followed in his father's footsteps as a musician, studying in Boston and Munich before joining the company in 1913. A year later, he married Lillian Houbertz, who had come to Bristol from Fultonville, New York, to teach a cooking course in the public schools. Together they had five children, including a boy they named after the first Wallace Barnes.

An accomplished pianist, Harry also played the clarinet, saxophone and cello, taking part in many community performances and musical shows. A small band he belonged to in the mid-1920s played on WTIC in Hartford the first night the station went on the air. In the 1930s Harry wrote many of his own
popular songs, regaling family and friends with such romantic ballads as "Painting My Lady's Picture" and "When My Sweetie Holds My Hand" ("My heart goes to beat the band").

"We tried to get Father to have them published, without success," his son Wally recalls. "Finally one day, at the ripe old age of nine or so, I decided to do something about it. I got on the daily train that used to run from Bristol through Waterbury to New York, bound for Scribner's with the sheet music in hand. I had told a friend of the family where I was going and swore her to secrecy. But of course as soon as I had left she felt she had to tell the family what I was up to.

"When I walked off the train in Grand Central, there was Bill Palmer, the senior partner in Dewey Ballantine, the company's law firm. 'Well, good morning, young man,' he said. 'What a surprise to see you here! What brings you to New York?' To make a long story short, he bought me lunch and put me on the train
back to Bristol. We never had Dad's music published."

Harry served as Associated Spring's Secretary from its incorporation in 1923 until 1941, when he was appointed First Vice President and General Manager of the Wallace Barnes, Dunbar and Manross divisions. He provided a valuable counterpoint to

his brother Fuller, who was more aggressive by nature and sometimes tended to be abrupt. Said one insider: "In business negotiations I suspect that Fuller, left to his own devices, might have turned off some people, but they worked together nicely as a team."

During his life in Bristol, Harry became prominent in local affairs, serving as a police commissioner and city councilman. Keenly interested in amateur athletics, he sponsored golf and tennis tournaments for the community's youth and donated land for use as an athletic field.

"Uncle Harry," as he was widely known, retired from the company's active management in 1954, but remained a member of the Board of Directors until his death in 1966. His name lives on in Bristol's Harry C. Barnes Memorial Nature Center, a 40-acre preserve and educational facility established in 1970 with the help of a gift from his widow Lillian, who passed away in 1986 at the age of 95.

greater endurance limit than any ever tested before. Apparently the bombardment toughened the steel, and even better results were obtained when small steel shot was substituted for grit as a conditioning medium..

As the company's magazine noted, "General Motors was equally excited by our laboratory results, ran their own tests, and shot-peening was off and running." Production lots of shot-peened springs were shipped in 1929. Zimmerli followed up with extensive experimentation and publication work, for which he later received the Sauveur Award of the American Society for Metals.

With the stock market crash of 1929, however, the era of progress and profits came to an end. Because of a sharp decline in automotive production, Associated Spring's two Michigan plants were particularly hard hit. In 1931, the company experienced a loss of $43,585; the next year, at the depth of the Great Depression, the loss increased more than tenfold to $482,925. Expanded facilities went unused, testing employee morale ("Idle machines and equipment do not create any uplift to one's spirits," one company official solemnly observed). In December, 1932, Fuller Barnes made a personal tour of all the plants, approving cost-cutting measures and reductions in wages and salaries paid to all employees. Though it wasn't a very nice Christmas present, it was something that had to be done.

Posters heralded the company's accomplishments in the 1940s. This one showed how the standard Army carbine depended on "our springs."

COMPANY HERO

Of all the Barnes men and women who served in the armed forces in World War II, probably the best remembered is Edward F. Wozenski of the Bristol steel mill, who became one of the most highly decorated officers in the Army of the United States.

A Bristol native and a 1937 graduate of the University of Connecticut, Wozenski joined the famed First Infantry Division as a first lieutenant in July, 1941, and participated with the "Big Red One" in all its engagements, including the initial Allied landings in Africa in 1942, the Sicily campaign in 1943 and the Normandy invasion in 1944.

At a critical point in Sicily, Captain Wozenski saved his army's right flank by singlehandedly routing an enemy tank attack on Hill 41, which was later named in his honor ("Upon him, for a tense while, the fate of the U.S. invasion rested," reported Time *magazine.) For various actions, Wozenski was awarded a chestful of medals, including two Distinguished Service Crosses, two Silver Stars, the Bronze Star, the Army Commendation Medal, the French Croix de Guerre, the Belgian Fourragere, the Combat Infantryman's Badge and several Presidential Unit Citations.*

On his return from the war, Colonel Wozenski commanded the 43rd Division's 169th Infantry Regiment, a National Guard unit composed largely of Bristolites, who were recalled to duty for the Korean conflict and stationed in Germany in the early 1950s. In 1967 he was promoted to Brigadier General in charge of the 43rd Divisional Command Headquarters, and in 1972 received the Army's Legion of Merit on his retirement after more than

"Big Ed" Wozenski

three decades of military service.

Ed Wozenski served his company with distinction as well, retiring as Supervisor of Finished Products for Associated Spring's Wallace Barnes Division. After his death in 1987, a full-dress ceremony was held in Bristol's National Guard Armory, including a personal tribute from Governor William O'Neill and the unveiling of a bronze memorial plaque with his portrait, donated by nearly 200 of Wozenski's former comrades in arms.

Said one of them in admiration: "A man like 'Big Ed' only comes our way once."

By 1933, business conditions had showed some improvement, and while earnings were slim at least the company was back in the black. Economic duress, meanwhile, had led spring-making companies to discuss ways of solving mutual problems. In August of that year 33 leading members of the industry met in Buffalo, New York, and elected Fuller F. Barnes President of a newly formed Spring Manufacturers Association (now the Spring Manufacturers Institute), a post he held from 1933 to 1941 and again from 1943 to 1946. Among other things, the association established a 40-hour work week and minimum hourly rates of 40 cents for males and 35 cents for females, a step forward that narrowed a longstanding gap.

Over the next few years it was decided that Associated Spring could operate more efficiently by turning its holding-company subsidiaries into operating divisions of a single corporation, a move that was accomplished in 1937. To round out its line of products, in the same year the company bought F. N. Manross & Sons, another old Bristol firm. Started by Frederick Manross, who had developed small springs for clocks and started manufacturing them in his kitchen in Forestville in 1882, it had become the nation's largest manufacturer of tiny hairsprings used in mechanical devices and instruments.

In 1939, storm clouds gathered again: in September, Germany invaded

Poland, setting the stage for another war. With the United States supplying much of the materiel as the "arsenal of democracy," and joining in the fray itself after Pearl Harbor in 1941, World War II would turn out to be far more widespread and destructive than any conflict in history. It would also be far more mechanized, requiring vast amounts of military hardware that depended on springs.

Beginning with the first war orders of the Lend-Lease program, all nine plants of Associated Spring pitched in. In Bristol, Barnes production lines made valve springs for engines that went into thousands of airplanes, tanks, trucks and Jeeps, while the rolling mill turned out steel for everything from band saws to machine-gun ammunition clips. Dunbar made holding springs for grenade launchers and flat springs to disperse aerial bombs from cluster racks; Manross produced fuse springs for artillery shells and hairsprings for instruments and gyroscopes. In Chicago, Gibson made springs for machine guns and spacer rings for land mines; in Corry, Raymond turned out springs for heavy artillery. Barnes's Canadian plant in Hamilton produced most of the recoil springs for the fast-firing Bofors antiaircraft cannon used aboard Navy ships.

All in all, the greatest effort involved the production of valve, clutch, starter and other springs for aircraft engines made by Pratt & Whitney, Wright, Allison, Rolls Royce, Jacobs and others, which powered everything from light training planes and artillery spotters to Vought Corsairs, Curtiss Helldivers, Lockheed Lightnings and giant Boeing Flying Fortresses. With the Bristol, Detroit and Ann Arbor plants leading the way, an estimated 90 per cent of all aircraft engine springs produced in World II were made by Associated Spring.

Recognition for the company's contributions came with the award of the coveted Army-Navy "E" to all its divisions

With many employees away at war in the early 1940s, women took over on the production lines at Associated Spring's plants.

at various times during the war; to add to the banners they flew proudly above their plants, both Barnes and Barnes-Gibson-Raymond received four additional stars for continuing excellence, Dunbar three and the other divisions two.

Beneath the flapping flags, it was evident that war, tragic as it was, had also resulted in a healthy spurt of industrial growth, helped by government contributions to expand needed manufacturing facilities. By the peak of production in 1943,

In the early 1940s, the Gibson Division in Chicago turned out an array of heavy-duty springs, referred to in company literature as "bouncing big brutes." Many would wind up in World War II vehicles and in recoil mechanisms for antiaircraft guns.

Associated Spring's total payroll had tripled from 2,000 to more than 6,000 employees, and shipments had reached an all-time high of $31 million. (Lest anyone get the wrong idea, one company official noted that the net after taxes that year, just under $1.4 million, could hardly be classified as war profiteering; two decades earlier, the firm had netted nearly that amount on peacetime sales of only one sixth as much.)

As they had in previous wars, many employees left the factory to take up the fight themselves. At the height of the conflict the Honor Rolls that were posted at the company's plants bore a total of 1,166 blue stars representing men and women who were away in the armed services—and gold stars for 23 others who would not come back.

Meanwhile, it fell to others to take their place on the production lines. In the Wallace Barnes plant in Bristol, where the workers had been predominantly male, females made up a good one third of the work force. As the company's magazine noted with a flourish, "Finger-nail-tinted hands manipulate machines that once were supposedly the exclusive realm of callous-palmed men." It marked the start of a new era in which women would work more as equals, not only on the factory floor, but increasingly in middle management, too.

In 1945, workers at Associated Spring's plants joined millions of other Americans in celebrating the long-awaited victories in Europe and Asia, parading and dancing in the streets while factory whistles blew, car horns blared and fireworks lit the sky. Then, as the euphoria faded, they settled down to business again. The company's work force, which had gradually declined toward the end of the war to slightly under 4,000, increased to 4,336 in the first full peacetime year of 1946. Due to pent-up consumer demands for springs, all plants were operating at or near capacity; sales were $22.9 million, compared with $13 million for 1940, the last peacetime year. The largest share, 35 percent, went to the automotive industry, with the electrical industry accounting for 15 percent, machinery 10 percent and hardware 7 percent. Because of a sharp reduction in the output of aircraft engines, sales to the aviation industry dropped to 2 percent from a wartime 38 percent.

The year 1946 was notable in two other respects.

With the removal of wartime controls on wages, the company tasted its first labor unrest. At the Gibson Division in Chicago, negotiations with the CIO's Steel Workers Union reached an impasse in January and a strike was called. The differences were later blamed on a mutual misunderstanding and in early April a contract was signed, but the experience left its mark.

Of broader significance to the company's future was a July meeting of Associated Spring's directors, who voted to increase the corporation's common stock from 270,000 to 725,000 shares—and for the first time to offer shares, through the over-the-counter market, to the public at large. An initial sale of 54,690 shares brought in nearly $1.6 million, which was set aside toward a proposed $2.5 million expansion of the Bristol steel mill at Forestville.

With this corporate milestone, an unusual aggregation of family-built and family-owned companies, largely used to doing business the old-fashioned way, entered a new and not entirely familiar world. While "going public" could provide needed funds for expansion and other advantages, it also meant that the company would have many more owners to answer to.

Not a few of them would be watching closely to see how well Associated Spring performed.

As officers salute, the Bristol plant receives the Army-Navy "E" award for its efforts in World War II.

BARNES-MADE SPRINGS

Engineered Pep and Power

Springs for every mechanical application

WALLACE BARNES COMPANY

DIVISION OF ASSOCIATED SPRING CORPORATION

BRISTOL, CONNECTICUT

C H A P T E R   F O U R

BROADENING THE BASE

*An advertisement bearing the Army-Navy "E" award
promises "pep and power" for the postwar years.*

When Detroit sneezed, we'd catch a cold.

— HAP BARNES

For Associated Spring, the postwar decades presented new technologies and new challenges, fueled by yet another economic boom. The company responded by launching into an exuberant expansion program around the country, highlighted in the 1960s by the acquisition of a large, and quite unfamiliar, distribution business, a stroke of genius that may have proved the company's salvation. In the 1970s growing confidence led to various adventures overseas, as well as the distribution of do-it-yourself retail hardware at home, experiments that were to meet with lesser success.

The company's initial building spree, largely a result of demand for new products after 15 years of depression and war, focused on bolstering its domestic leadership in springs. As a glance at "Historical Highlights" in the back of this book shows, the activity was intense—a new spring-making Ohio Division and a new building for Raymond in 1947; a major addition to the Forestville steel mill in 1949; a new Milwaukee Division and Cleveland Sales Office in 1950; a big plant for BGR near Detroit in 1951. The dream of a coast-to-coast operation became a reality in 1952 with the acquisition of a small but thriving manufacturer in Los

Angeles, Seaboard Coil Spring Corp.

Meanwhile, things were not going quite so smoothly behind the scenes. As family businesses sometimes do as they move from one generation to the next, Barnes had run into personal problems, though the differences were ultimately resolved. The issue was a basic one: Who was going to run the company?

Carlyle F. ("Hap") Barnes, President Fuller Barnes's son, had gone to work for the company in 1948, after graduating from Wesleyan University, and had risen from staff assistant in the Bristol Division to General Manager in 1951. His cousin Wallace ("Wally") Barnes, two years younger and the son of First Vice President Harry Barnes, was flying as a commercial pilot and had started his own nonscheduled airline, Nutmeg Air Transport, while graduating cum laude from Williams College in 1949 and from Yale Law School in 1952.

Hap's father, Fuller, whose health was deteriorating, wanted to see his son ensconced as President before he died. Wally's side of the family pushed their own choice; failing that, they urged that Fuller's second in command, a well qualified executive who was not a member of the family, be named instead. Tempers

Under the motto "The Critical Parts People," the company has provided everything from blade locks for jet engines (above) to high-strength construction bolts (below).

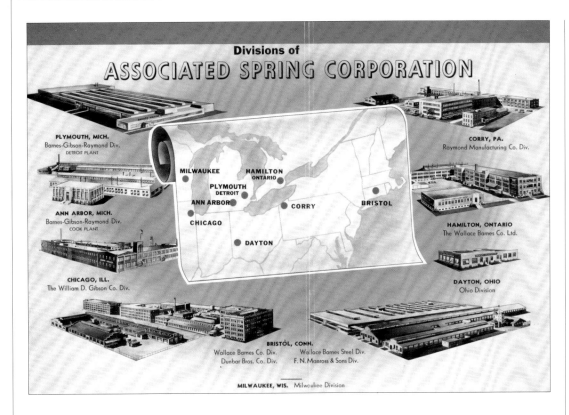

A composite view of Associated Spring's plants in 1950.

flared, a participant recalls, and there was more than one shouting match.

At the time Wally was thinking of a future with a New York law firm, but under family pressure he joined the company, as all Barneses were expected to do. Within three weeks on the job, however, he had a falling out with his uncle. Wally quit and went to work for a Bristol law office, Beach & Calder, where he was to remain for a decade.

In 1953, Hap Barnes took over as President of ASC; his father, Fuller, continued as Chairman, passing away two years later. Hap found that ASC's five divisions had been operating pretty much as their managers liked. At the urging of his financial officer, Roland Sylvester, he instituted a common accounting system and sent the executives to the American Management Association's training school.

Hap soon reached out for his cousin and childhood playmate to come aboard. In 1957, Wally Barnes—who had been doing a growing business with the company as an outside counsel and was also a member of the board—joined ASC as its Secretary. In 1962, giving up his law practice, he was elected Executive Vice President and went to work for the company full time.

Despite the family contretemps, the company had continued to grow, exceeding sales of $50 million a year. It had also begun to make its first tentative moves to explore markets abroad.

In 1957 a small plant was opened in Puerto Rico to manufacture simple double-looped extension springs for various products, taking advantage of favorable tax laws and wages there (the plant was closed within four years, the victim of technological advances on the mainland and a need for shorter delivery times). Two years later ASC, believing Argentina to be the single most promising country in Latin America, combined with local businessmen to form Resortes Argentina S.A. in Cordoba, which manufactured springs for a growing automotive market there. At the same time the company started to probe possibilities in Europe and Asia. In 1961 an affiliation was made with Tempered Group Ltd. in Sheffield, England, makers of springs, saw blades and other products. In 1962 Hap and Wally Barnes set out on an 11-day tour of industrial plants in Japan. They were impressed by the engineering ingenuity and degree of automation achieved by the Japanese, particularly at NHK Spring Co. of Yokohama, Japan's largest spring maker. Though they were unable to conclude

The 1954 launching of U.S.S. Nautilus, the world's first atomic-powered submarine, was of more than passing interest to employees of Associated Spring. She contained some 140 different types of ASC springs at critical points within her long, sleek hull.

a joint venture with NHK, they planted seeds for future collaboration that would bear fruit in the 1980s.

The next two years were marked by events that would alter the course of the company's history.

In 1963 Associated Spring, whose stock had been traded over the counter for 17 years, was listed on the New York Stock Exchange, under the call letters "AAS." By now some 5,200 shareholders owned 1,143,025 shares of Associated's common stock. To encourage its employees to share in that ownership, the directors approved a Monthly Investment Plan that would permit workers to purchase stock through payroll deductions, with the company paying the brokerage fees.

ASC continued its foreign adventures in 1964 with the acquisition of three

Workers of the Bowman Auto Supply Company fill orders in their Cleveland distribution center in 1934.

small companies in Mexico, Resortes Mecanicos S.A. and Resortes Industriales del Norte, makers of springs and other metal products, and Cuchilleria Imperial, a manufacturer of knives, scissors and other cutlery.

The same year Hap Barnes was elected Chairman and Chief Executive Officer, Wally President and Chief Operating Officer. The move formalized what had become a close working relationship between the cousins, who were now functioning as a team.

The real watershed, however, came later in 1964 when the company "swallowed hard," as Wally Barnes remembers, and jumped into a completely new field. Up to that point all ASC's acquisitions had been related to springs, but by the early 1960s it had become clear that springs could be a very cyclical business. "We were 50 percent or more dependent on the automotive industry," says Wally, "and as that industry went through its cy-

A pretty greeter in nautical garb welcomes visitors to an early exhibit of Bowman's marine products.

cles, we were being whipsawed." As Hap Barnes put it: "Every time Detroit sneezed, we caught a cold."

While ASC officials were pondering this fundamental problem, Clarke Simonds, an investment banker and partner of G. H. Walker & Co. in Providence, Rhode Island, came to the company with a notion that seems almost brilliant in retrospect: If you want to lessen your dependence on the original equipment business, get into a field that is more tied to the replacement and overhaul market; in times when people hesitate to invest in new cars or other machines, they tend to spend more money maintaining and repairing their old ones. Distribution companies, Simonds also pointed out, can be very profitable—often more so than manufacturing ones.

The officers agreed to look at several candidates, which were screened by Edwin V. Ladd, Jr., Corporate Secretary and General Counsel. The leading one was The Bowman Products Company of Cleveland, which had started as a small operation in 1927 furnishing repair items to automobile dealers and service garages; it had incorporated as The Bowman Auto Supply Company in 1934 before adopting its current name in 1944. Bowman was a family-owned company until 1960, when 40 percent of its shares were made available on the over-the-counter market.

Under the guidance of its principal stockholders, Chairman Charles Devine and Chief Executive Officer Lyle

ALL IN THE FAMILY

Paul Keyowski, Joan Keyowski, Jeff Twombly, Eleanor Twombly.

It *is not unusual in the Barnes corporate family, particularly in the longer-established divisions, for employees to work for the company for 30, 40 or even 50 years. Nor is it exceptional for children to follow in a parent's footsteps: in Bristol and Corry, several families have spanned three generations at Barnes, starting before the turn of the century.*

In more than one instance, family members carry on the tradition simultaneously. At Barnes Group headquarters, Eleanor Twombly is a senior secretary, her brother Paul Keyowski serves as maintenance coordinator and Paul's wife Joan works in the payroll department. Both Eleanor's son, Jeff Twombly, and Paul's daughter, Ann Marie Fippinger, are employed in the Bris-

tol Spring Division across the street. Earlier family members at the same location were Eleanor and Paul's mother, Bertha "Betty" Keyowski, who had over 22 years of service, and Anna Twombly, Eleanor's mother-in-law, who worked at the Bristol plant for more than 30 years.

The prize for family togetherness, however, probably goes to the Williamses of England, who comprise half the staff of Motalink's distribution depot in North Wales. Ian Williams is branch manager; his brother Glen serves as engineering sales representative. Ian's wife, Norma, handles inquiries and secretarial duties. Norma's father, Noel Hughes, acts as clerk, watching over the rest of the family and keeping their thriving depot properly stocked.

To withstand critical stresses, a roller coaster at California's Magic Mountain uses Bowman Distribution's "Bowmalloy" bolts.

Thoburn, Bowman had seen the virtues of diversification, and had gradually added to its line other maintenance products for truck-fleet, contractor, marine and industrial customers. By the time the company came to the attention of Associated Spring, automotive supplies, once 100 percent of its business, accounted for about half of its sales of $18 million a year.

To its would-be suitors in Bristol, Bowman was a different kettle of fish. Unlike Associated, it did not make its own products; it bought them from other manufacturers, screening them first for quality and dependability, then repackaged them under the Bowman label and sold them to industrial users—not through the usual route of jobbers but through more than 400 sales representatives who worked on commission for Bowman alone.

Though both Bowman and its competitors priced their products slightly lower than maintenance and replacement parts offered directly by manufacturers, Bowman pitched its prime selling advantage not on price but on the valuable services its agents performed. Bowman promised to reduce its clients' headaches by cutting through the confusion of ordering from different suppliers, and not knowing where a given item was when it was needed (before Bowman came in, the average customer's stock room "looked like the Black Hole of Calcutta," one executive remarked). Through its agents, the company guaranteed to anticipate its clients' needs and to keep their parts bins neatly organized and automatically stocked.

At the time, Bowman offered more than 13,000 items: pumps, mufflers, brake parts, seat belts, mirrors, clips, springs and other products for automobiles; marine hardware, safety flares, boat horns and seat cushions for pleasure craft; and a wide range of nuts, bolts, screws and other fasteners for general industrial use. To distribute all these bits

pany to go deeply in debt, something that as an old Yankee institution it had always tried desperately to avoid.

On the brighter side, Bowman would enhance the company's marketing expertise, an area in which, almost everyone agreed, it could use some help. Even more important, the move could reduce Associated's dependence on the annual production rate of new cars into which its valve springs and other products went. Bowman's "aftermarket" business, in fact,

Valve springs made by the company, and other products, such as fasteners, distributed by Bowman, are used in racing cars on the NASCAR circuit, in the Indianapolis "500"– and in millions of passenger automobiles.

and pieces in timely fashion, Bowman had 500 employees working in a large warehouse in Cleveland, which earlier in the century had been an auto-making plant, and in smaller leased space in Oakland, Dallas and Toronto.

To ASC's officers and directors, Bowman posed an interesting dilemma. Charlie Devine wanted out, for $15 million cash. Buying him, however, would not only represent a radical departure from the basic spring-making business Barnes had grown used to for more than a century. It would also require the com-

tended to run in cycles opposite to those of the new-car trade, promising to level out the valleys that had long deviled ASC.

"It was a business that we knew nothing about," says Wally Barnes. "And it was the first time that the company had ever considered borrowing that kind of money. It was a big sell as far as many of the directors were concerned."

The net of it was that the company put up $3.9 million in cash, took out a $12 million, 20-year loan, and bought all 728,242 shares of outstanding Bowman stock for $15,657,203, including owner-

Architects of the company's expansion in the 1960s (from left): Wally Barnes, Roland ("Syl") Sylvester, Ed Ladd, Fred Crist, Hap Barnes.

The Big Leap worked. In fact, it changed the company forever, and in terms of earnings, for the good. Bowman now contributes nearly half the corporation's sales, and a hefty piece of its profits as well.

"Bowman has contributed in a very significant way not only to the growth and strength of this company but to its very survival," says Wally Barnes. "If we hadn't had Bowman, we probably wouldn't have had the resources to expand into the aerospace business, or to make some of the Associated Spring investments that we've made."

Those investments continued with renewed vigor, helped in no small measure by Bowman-generated cash. In 1965, Bowman itself opened new distribution centers in Atlanta, Georgia, and Union, New Jersey, and established Bowman S.A. de C.V. in Mexico City. The following year, after investigations by Wally Barnes and Ed Ladd in Europe, ASC acquired Tevema Fabriek van Technische Veeren N.V. of Amsterdam, The Netherlands, a leading maker of precision mechanical springs with 175 employees and annual sales of $1.5 million. The company also bought Broadbent & Co., Ltd. of Rochdale, England, manufacturers of springs, wire products, a patented lawn aerator and a folding baby carriage, with 160 employees and sales of $600,000 a year.

ship of Bowman and its subsidiaries, the Spirex Screw Co. of Akron, Ohio, and Bowman Products (Canada) Ltd. ASC kept on Thoburn as President and General Manager of its new Bowman Products Division, with Devine retiring comfortably but continuing to act as a consultant. The deal was completed on December 15, 1964, in time to celebrate Christmas.

"It was a big leap, requiring new marketing and financial savvy," recalls Jerry McQuillan, who arrived at ASC as Manager of Marketing just about the time the deal was being done. A Bostonian with a bachelor's degree from Holy Cross, an MBA from Harvard and 16 years of experience with General Electric, the market-wise McQuillan was to go on to become the company's President—the first professional manager outside the Barnes family to achieve that post.

At home, meanwhile, ASC was building new plants in Milwaukee, Chicago, Asheville, North Carolina, and Ann

HAP BARNES

When Carlyle F. ("Hap") Barnes retired in 1989 after 41 years with the company, everyone at the party wore little plastic firemen's hats, sang "Thanks for the Memories" and roared at a slide show of "This is Your Life." Hap's trademark grin grew even wider when he was presented with not one but two model fire engines—which had been made largely out of nuts, bolts and springs by admirers at Bowman and Associated Spring.

The mementos are proudly displayed in Hap's house in Bristol, where he maintains a veritable museum of firefighting paraphernalia from around the world, including scores of fancy helmets, brass nozzles, alarm boxes, fire axes and firehouse gongs. In a nearby garage are two full-sized fire engines, one a 1928 hose truck that has seen better days, the other a 1936 American LaFrance that he keeps well polished and often drives around, giving children rides or joining in town parades. ("There's a lot of little boy in him," his wife Betty confides.)

Being a fire buff runs in the family for Hap Barnes: his great-great-grandfather Alphonso was one of the founders of Bristol's fire department well over a century ago. Hap himself has been a Bristol fire commissioner for 34 years, and still responds to calls on two-way radios he has installed in his house and car (in the car trunk are extinguishers and resuscitation equipment, which he has used more than once). Now that he is retired, he has more time to tinker around with his engines and enlarge his collection of memorabilia, both of which he loves to do.

The other main love in Hap Barnes's life—besides Betty, three grown daughters and a son—has been the family company. While he was a boy at Loomis School in Windsor, Connecticut (where he was President of the Student Council and won the school's award for "Industry, Loyalty and Manliness"), he worked summers in the Bristol plant as an office boy and truck driver. After graduating from Wesleyan in 1948 (where he captained the fencing team, and first started chasing fires), Hap became a trainee in the Wallace Barnes Division, rising to General Manager in 1951. Two years later, at age 29, he was elected President of the company, serving in that role for 11 years. He then took over for 13 years as Chairman and CEO before going on to head the Board's Executive Committee for another 12 years, a post he still holds.

Concern for others has been evident in his work for the Bristol Hospital, the family's Barnes Foundation and other charitable and educational organizations, including St. Lawrence University and the McDuffie School. The same concern has also been a mark of his career with the company, where employees appreciated his habit of getting out on the factory floor whenever possible to say hello and find out what was going on—an effective technique known as "management by walking around."

Hap in a toy car with his sister Aurelia ("Re"), and in his fire engine today.

Arbor, Michigan, while the Bowman Division laid plans for a new distribution centers in Edmonton, Alberta, and Rockford, Illinois. The company also acquired the Frank Holister Co. of Dallas, manufacturer of concrete reinforcement accessories and custom metal parts for the oil industry, with factories in Dallas, Houston, Tulsa, Denver and Memphis, 320 employees and annual sales of $6 million.

In 1968 ASC became a $100 million company, posting record sales of $108,562,691.

To help bring its diverse businesses under the same tent, the company had begun to stress a new motto: "Service by Design." A forerunner of the company's "Guiding Philosophy" (Chapter 6), it emphasized that the nature of all ASC operations required "a high input of ingenuity and innovation," and that it strived to be "a very personal kind of company because people, not machines, provide these critical ingredients." Unlike some others that advertised themselves as "people companies" to polish their corporate images, ASC really meant it; with virtually every batch a custom order, it had to rely on people in designing its products and services to meet client needs.

As the 1970s opened, the Associated Spring Corporation stood at a new pinnacle, with close to 6,000 employees in 41 locations in the U.S. and abroad, and nearly 1.9 million shares of stock outstanding.

The company celebrated by popping a cork or two, and getting itself listed on the London Stock Exchange.

At about the same time, ground was broken for the company's largest building project to date, and the largest spring-making plant in the United States: a modern, $5 million, 221,000-square-foot factory for the Wallace Barnes Division in Bristol. To be erected on land that had been cleared by the city for downtown redevelopment, the sprawling, air-conditioned, almost windowless structure would replace most of the older plant buildings that stood a stone's throw from the site of the wooden factory where the first Wallace Barnes started in 1857. As part of the deal, the City of Bristol provided $500,000 worth of utilities and other site improvements; in return, it received a shiny new anchor for its massive urban renewal effort, which had been faltering for several years.

Through the decade, overseas expansion went on as Barnes warmed to its multinational role. In 1971, ASC acquired STECE AB Industrifjadrar of Montseras, Sweden, a major supplier of springs, stampings and related products to Northern European markets, with 400 employees and $6 million in annual sales. The same year it also bought Herbert Terry & Sons Ltd. of Redditch, England, producer of springs, stampings, hose clips and lamps, with 950 employees and $5 million in sales.

Within two years Barnes had added new foreign arms to its Bowman Distribution Group as well: Motalink Ltd. of Corsham, England, which brought in some $4 million a year distributing automotive and construction maintenance parts by means of its own vans through the British Isles, and a similar but smaller company, Autoliaisons of France.

In 1974, ASC went back to South America, acquiring Indap S.A. of São

ed Spring" no longer filled the bill. The name was changed to Barnes Group Inc.—the word "group" chosen to suggest the largely autonomous manner in which each of its components functioned. Unchanged was the distinctive logo that Associated had adopted, an abstract letter "A" with a springlike curlicue inside (or a "snail in a tent," as some referred to it

An employee of England's Motalink Ltd. delivers maintenance and repair products to a customer from the back of his van. The company was acquired by Barnes in 1973, along with a similar distributor in France.

Paulo, Brazil, a $4-million-a-year maker of custom metal parts. Two years later, it bought out the West German firm of Stumpp & Schuele, a major supplier of springs to the German automotive industry, along with its Brazilian operation and 30 percent of its subsidiary in India. By now, it seems, the old Yankee company had grown more accustomed to living with debt.

In 1976, the company's officers and directors surveyed their increasingly diverse empire and decided that "Associat-

less reverently).

By now Hap Barnes had served as the company's chief executive for two decades, and the time seemed ripe for a change of family roles. In 1977, Wallace Barnes took over the duty as Chairman of the Board and CEO, while Hap remained a senior officer of the company and became Chairman of the Executive Committee. Jeremiah McQuillan moved up as President and Chief Operating Officer, and Edwin Ladd was elected Senior Vice President for Finance and Law.

Seeking new ways to enlarge its distribution business at home, Barnes Group next acquired Globe Industries, Inc., a major distributor of do-it-yourself automobile replacement parts and other hardware to the retail market, with warehouses in Lincoln, Rhode Island, and Atlanta, Georgia. Feeding to Caldor, Zayre, Bradlees and other mass merchandising chains, Globe, in effect, acted as a purchasing agent and stocker for the hardware and automotive accessories section of their stores, providing them with any selection of 5,000 different items as required. Founded in 1935, the company had sales of $37 million in 1977, up sharply, and attractively, from $9 million five years before. Barnes Group purchased Globe in 1978 for $16.7 million in cash and notes. As had been the case with most other acquisitions, former owners, Howard and Arnold Kaufman, were kept on as the key managers of Barnes's new Globe Distribution business.

Bowman agent Paul Pfeffer checks repair and replacement parts with Sherm Palan of Rand McNally Co. in Taunton, Mass. Items are stocked in a meticulously organized "Bowman System" of bins and trays.

What was needed now was a proper flagship for the fleet, and a suitable home for a growing management staff that had been overflowing a building erected back in World War I. On July 19, 1979, the Barnes Group invited employees and local dignitaries to celebrate the opening of its new international headquarters in downtown Bristol, a strikingly modern, $3 million structure designed around a skylighted atrium and circular staircase three stories high. Located diagonally across the street from the big new spring factory, the building occupied another area that had been cleared for urban renewal but that had remained a vacant, dust-blown eyesore for almost a decade until the company stepped in to help realize the city's downtown dreams.

Continuing its strategy of "balanced

expansion," Barnes followed with two more additions in the distribution field. Early in 1979 it acquired, for $2.5 million, The Chanenson Corp. of South Holland, Illinois, a $7 million-a-year distributor of automotive replacement parts and other hardware items, serving Midwestern retail outlets much as Globe did Eastern ones. The second acquisition, for $8.1 million, was Pioneer Products Inc. of Meridian, Mississippi, a distributor of products to automotive clutch and engine rebuilders, with sales of $11 million-plus a year.

To round out the decade, the company put on a final burst, announcing a $5.2 million expansion of its Burlington, Ontario, factory to serve fast-growing automotive and other industrial markets in Canada. Also scheduled were a new Globe distribution center in Gainesville, Georgia, to supply mass retailers in the South, and a $5 million plant for Stumpp & Schuele to provide valve and other springs for the growing automobile industry in Brazil.

All in all, it had been a bravura performance for nearly 35 years. Barnes Group finished the 1970s with its eighth consecutive year of record growth, reaching annual sales of $431,495,000—a 300 percent rise in both sales and earnings per share.

The figure earned the company 480th place in the "Fortune 500" list of top industrial corporations, the first time it had entered that magic circle of American enterprise.

Descending a spiral staircase in a skylighted court, visitors inspect Barnes Group's new international headquarters in Bristol on its opening in 1979.

CHAPTER FIVE

SHARPENING THE FOCUS

At Central Metal Products in East Windsor, Connecticut,
Ron Andrews checks an engine seal on a coordinate measuring
machine to ensure the accuracy of its dimensions.

*We used to think bigger was better. Now we
know it's better to be the best—and the most profitable.*

— WALLY BARNES

*Critical
components
for commercial
jet engines and
helicopter engines
are produced from
a wide range of
exotic space alloys
by Central Metal
Products' precision-
machining unit.*

As the 1980s dawned, Barnes Group began looking toward new horizons: exploding Asian markets overseas, and the burgeoning aerospace field at home. It also made some painful decisions to cut its losses, and to focus more sharply on profitability in order to survive as a company.

At the beginning of the decade it was evident that Asia would supply an increasing share of global automotive, electronic and other needs, and that Barnes would do well to share in its growth. In May, 1980, CEO Wallace Barnes, one of 17 delegates on a Connecticut trade mission to the People's Republic of China, had a chance to test the waters first hand.

Following his trip, a "Far East Task Force" was formed to develop new opportunities in the Pacific; the group, headed by Clarence Fauntleroy, Group Vice President for Associated Spring, recommended establishing a beachhead in Singapore. The next year construction started on a 24,000-square-foot pilot plant that would provide a full range of springs and metal stampings to manufacturers of electronic equipment, cameras, calculators and other products in Singapore, Malaysia, Indonesia, Taiwan and Hong Kong. Meanwhile, continuing its Euro-

pean expansion, the company had acquired a sizeable spring-maker in France, Herckelbout-Dawson et Fils, with $27 million in annual sales.

Signs of basic trouble, however, began surfacing in 1981. Barnes's sales had grown to $463 million and the number of its employees had risen to an all-time high of just over 7,000, but net income plummeted from $24 million to $5 million in a single year. The situation would worsen in 1982, when a recession contributed to a humiliating loss of $5.5 million for Associated Spring and $2.7 million for the company as a whole—the first red ink it had seen since the Great Depression of the early 1930s.

One person who didn't like what he saw was A. Stanton Wells, the company's Vice President for Finance, who had come over from Xerox a couple of years before. Stan Wells looked agonizingly at the books. He also spent a lot of time trying to convince Wally Barnes that the company couldn't go on as it was, making everything for everybody without making much money for itself.

One of the things that needed changing was the company's effort in Europe, where its adopted cousins weren't pulling their weight.

"We had hoped for synergy among our European partners, the way our companies worked in the U.S.," says Wallace Barnes. "That just didn't happen. We ran into different languages, different currencies, different customs. National boundaries still meant a lot.

"Basically, the Germans didn't want to buy from the French, the French didn't want to buy from the English, the English didn't want to buy from the Swedes, and no one really wanted to buy from the Americans either, no matter what the product was. Company purchasing officers had long-established contacts with their suppliers—the old-boy network, hunting lodges and all the rest. We couldn't get our people to cooperate, to sell outside their own countries, even though we knew the market was there."

Adds Hap Barnes: "The much-heralded 'Common Market' just didn't materialize; perhaps we were ahead of our time. It got to the point where we couldn't see any light at the end of the tunnel. We thought we'd better get out."

And so the company began an organized retreat, with the board of directors approving the full or partial divestiture of its manufacturing holdings in Europe, starting with those in Sweden and the Netherlands. It also threw in the towel on Indap in Brazil, Resortes Argentina in Argentina and Cuchilleria Imperial in Mexico, which were also marginally profitable or poorly matched with the company's overall plans for growth. Retained were the company's

At Associated Spring's automated valve-spring plant in Saline, Michigan, Technician Linda Brier and Quality Engineer Bob Zill, aided by a computer, inspect springs coming off the production line.

van-distribution businesses in England and France, which remained profitable, as well as its spring-making subsidiary in Mexico and the Stumpp & Schuele operation in Brazil.

The following year the company retrenched further by closing Associated Spring's Plymouth, Michigan plant, which for several years had been experiencing heavy losses because of depressed conditions in the automotive industry and a serious overcapacity among parts suppliers. In 1983, faced with a loss of $5 million in its remaining European plants, Barnes sold its spring operations in England, Germany and France. Confronted by continuing overcapacity and weak markets at home, the company also made a decision to shut down its spring-making plants in Mattoon and Lombard, Illinois, and Pointe Claire, Quebec, affecting a total of some 150 employees. In all, the divestitures resulted in a before-tax write-off of $16 million. They left scars, to be sure, but they also left the company in leaner condition to push ahead.

While making these unaccustomed and uncomfortable decisions, Barnes had already moved toward a brighter future in the air. It was still selling parts for conventional propeller aircraft, as it had been for more than half a century, but that market had sharply diminished as jets and spacecraft had moved to the fore. A share in the new business of "aerospace," moreover, promised higher profit margins than the company's traditional spring-manufacturing business, and a chance to increase its overall technical capabilities as well.

Once again Clarke Simonds, now a vice president of Drexel Burnham Lambert and a member of Barnes's Board of Directors, put some ideas on the table. For openers, he suggested looking at the purchase of Central Metal Products, located not far away in East Windsor, Connecticut.

Central Metal, with some 50 employees and sales of $10.5 million, was turning out 500 different kinds of precision metal parts on custom order, most of them for jet engines (its major customer was Pratt & Whitney in nearby East Hartford, among the biggest in the field). Arnold Thompson and Rodney Reynolds, who had started the firm in 1972 with a handful of people and built it into a sizeable operation with a 25,000-square-foot plant, agreed to a purchase price of $14.4 million, and to stay on as managers of the company. In 1981, Central Metal Products became the first unit of Barnes's new Aerospace Group.

A second and larger member of the group came aboard the following year, when Barnes acquired the Windsor Manufacturing Company of Windsor, Connecticut, a maker and refurbisher of components for the aircraft, airline and aerospace industries with several hundred employees and sales of $27 million a year. Windsor con-

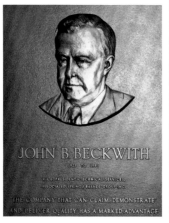

The company's coveted Beckwith Award, given to Associated Spring divisions that excel in quality. A respected industry leader who served Barnes for 35 years, Beckwith was Vice President of Technical Services when he died in 1981.

sisted of two separate but related operations. Its manufacturing division provided precision-machined parts to major customers such as Pratt & Whitney, Avco Lycoming, Sikorsky, Kaman and Rolls Royce. Its Windsor Airmotive Division had become a leading specialist in the overhaul and repair of jet engine components, with 20 major airlines and the military as clients. Walter Rose and Paul D'Arcy, who had started the company in 1950 and were principal stockholders, negotiated the sale for $29 million plus $3.8 million in real estate. Some of Windsor's key executives agreed to continue in their management roles.

With these realignments, and a general economic upturn, in 1984 Barnes Group was back in the black. Profits at Associated Spring were especially encouraging, rebounding from a loss to more than $15 million in earnings. Much of the improvement at Associated was due to a new program of Statistical Quality Control, which committed employees and managers to checking and adjusting output, preventing defects and "making it right the first time."

In connection with the program, an annual John B. Beckwith Memorial Award was established to recognize the division that posted the greatest improvement in quality each year. Named for the company's late Vice President of Technical Services, who had been a respected leader in the industry, it was first awarded to the Wallace Barnes Co., Ltd. of Burlington, Ontario, which was

A BOWMAN AGENT'S DAY

Mike Carter of Shelton, Connecticut, is an early riser. He gets up each weekday morning around 5, lets out the dogs, makes breakfast, then settles down to an hour of paperwork, faxing orders to Bowman Distribution's warehouse in Edison, New Jersey. Then he climbs into the family van to start his rounds, which include some 70 regular customers in New Haven and Fairfield counties along Connecticut's coast.

Carter, a slim, soft-spoken man of 47, is one of Bowman's nearly 900 independent sales agents, who, through 12 distribution and customer service centers, provide 60,000 industrial and transportation firms in North America with more than 22,000 different products they depend on every day—nuts, bolts, screws, anchors, rivets; drill bits, saw blades, grinding wheels; spray paints, cleaners, adhesives, lubricants; automotive, electrical, welding, plumbing and general maintenance supplies.

This morning, welcoming a visitor along for the ride, Mike starts with NRS Carting in Norwalk, a new client, consulting with the foreman on the best configuration and location for Bowman's distinctive blue cabinets of bins and drawers, which he will soon deliver, install and keep stocked with all the necessities to maintain the company's fleet of garbage trucks.

Next he calls on the Norwalk Company, a manufacturer of air and gas compressors, one of the larger, established clients

that he services on a set day each week. Lugging Bowman's suitcase-like catalog binder ("It's heavy, so you shift hands a lot"), he greets the receptionist, dropping a handful of Chiclet packages with the Bowman logo on her desk.

Proceeding to the factory floor, Carter chats with the manager like an old friend, then collects shipments that have arrived UPS from Edison, slits the cartons open and dumps the contents of each smaller box into the proper pigeonholes. While he's at it, he stuffs a couple of handfuls of peppermints, also packaged with the Bowman logo, into empty bins where employees will find them when they go to pick up supplies. ("It must be Tuesday," cracks a nearby worker. "Time for after-dinner mints.")

The third stop is Showtech, Inc., which Carter especially enjoys because it's one of his more colorful customers—a leading maker of stage settings for Broadway shows like Starlight Express as well as movie sets, animated sculptures and huge advertising displays. Waving to a couple of carpenters, he hunkers down to check his bins, replenishes near-empty ones and writes up fresh needs on his order pad. He then cross-checks invoices against receipts in the offices upstairs ("They're a little behind, and I don't mind pitching in.")

After a bite of lunch, Carter will call on three or four more clients, including his

CONTINUED

CONTINUED

largest, Schick in Milford, which uses a lot of his bolts in injection molds for its plastic razors. He arrives home around 6 to collapse for half an hour in his whirlpool spa, which takes the kinks out after a day on the road. Then he settles down to a quiet dinner with his wife, more paperwork and early to bed.

To Mike Carter and other Bowman agents, organization is the name of the game. "You wouldn't believe the mess in a lot of stock rooms," he says. "No one knows where anything is, and they send someone down to the hardware store every other day—often to buy something they already have, except they don't know it because it's buried somewhere."

With the "Bowman System," Carter and his counterparts not only organize the myriad bits and pieces into a visible, accessible order; they also provide a lot of extra services that their competitors don't. "We clean out the old mess, and give them credit against future orders for their usable stuff," he says. "We provide free cabinets with labels tailored to their supplies. We come back at regular intervals to check and order what they need, without their having to worry about it. We give them an 18-month warranty on materials and labor for anything they buy from us. We eliminate the headaches, the nuisances. You just go to the bin and it's there."

Since they act as independent entrepreneurs, Bowman agents have the flexibility to

tailor their programs and levels of service to the particular needs of each customer. In determining a customer's needs, Carter emphasizes the importance of establishing an effective partnership between agent and client. The result is usually that the client's plant maintenance becomes more efficient and more productive.

"Our programs are designed to enhance the bottom line for the customer," he says. "As partners, we get to know each other, and this leads to a better modus operandi.

"I often tell a client, sure, someone can walk in the door tomorrow and offer you a lower

price, but how long can he live on that without giving you poor service or inching up his price? Bowman's relations with its customers are built on providing superior service. That's the real key to success."

In an atmosphere of intense competition, Carter has found that gaining a new prospect's confidence, and getting his first order, can take as many as six or eight in-person calls.

Like any good salesman, Carter knows the value of the personal approach: "Before you can sell your products, you have to sell yourself. The customer has to like you as a person. He has to be able to trust you to deliver,

without having to keep an eye on you all the time. You have to be patient; you have to be persistent. And you have to be honest."

In his five years with Bowman, these simple precepts have paid off: Carter has built up a substantial, and loyal, clientele (with occasional assists from his district manager, Henry Day, in paving the way on larger accounts). With commissions on more than $400,000 in annual sales, he is earning a comfortable living; as a bonus, he has been twice named his district's "Agent of the Year" and has gone on several of the company's annual "Quota Busters" trips, including weeklong vacations to places like Hawaii and the Caribbean provided to star performers and their wives. Nevertheless, he is a bit concerned about meeting his current sales goals because of a general business slump.

"Of course there are risks in this kind of business," he observes. "You're working strictly on commission—only beginning agents get a draw—and if you don't sell, you don't eat. When you take a holiday or vacation, no one's paying you, and if you break a leg or something and are out for six weeks, you have a health plan to fall back on but your income grinds to a halt."

At the same time, there are the challenges, and the rewards. Says Mike Carter with a grin: "It's the next best thing to running your own company, without having to raise the capital to get it off the ground."

cited for a 46 percent cost reduction in making high-quality products and a 61 percent drop in customer returns. Inscribed on the plaque were Beckwith's own words, which said it all: "The company that can claim, demonstrate and deliver quality has a marked advantage over the competition."

At the same time Barnes recognized that achieving high quality on a continuing basis can work only if everyone is involved, most importantly the workers on the factory floor—and if they are constantly motivated to come up with better ideas. To decentralize its decision-making and eliminate red tape, the company launched a new initiative in which senior executives of all units were encouraged to adopt a more "entrepreneurial" style, which it hoped would foster a greater sense of ownership, risk-taking and responsibility for results.

To help implement Barnes's new management style, a nominating committee of the Board of Directors — headed by Richard LeBlond, Vice Chairman of New York's Chemical Bank, and aided by executive recruiters at Korn, Ferry & Co.— launched a year-long search for a new President and Chief Operating Officer to replace Jerry McQuillan, who was soon to retire at the age of 65. Again, Barnes looked outside, though there were two younger family members on the board ("You don't attract and retain the best professional managers to run your business if they think their way to the top is going to blocked by family con-

siderations," says Wally Barnes.)

Chosen was William R. Fenoglio, who took over on January 1, 1985. A 45-year-old native of Clinton, Indiana, with a degree in mechanical engineering, Fenoglio had served General Electric in various management capacities for 23 years, most recently as Vice President and General Manager of GE's Component Motor Division, where he had been responsible for 28 domestic and offshore operations

Heng Chun Kwang makes air coils for electronic components at Associated Spring's plant in Singapore, which sells its products in the Far East, Europe and the United States. The plant boasts the largest inventory of precision springs in the Pacific.

with 14,000 employees and close to $1 billion in annual sales.

Fenoglio's first year on the job was not without problems. By now, profits at the company's Globe Distribution Group had been in a two- or three-year slide. Its large chain-store clients, pressured by sluggish sales, had begun to shift away from do-it-yourself hardware toward more profitable wearing apparel and other "soft" lines, and to deal directly with manufacturers rather than through distributors. Globe had tried to counter by bolstering its own offerings with new lines of paint products, unpainted furniture and lawn and garden supplies, but the general slump was leading mass merchandisers to cut their inventories and even close down stores. The officers and directors finally decided to call it quits in

the retail business, and to concentrate on areas of greater promise. In 1985 Globe was sold to a group of private investors for $16.9 million in cash and assumed debt, leaving Barnes Group with a before-tax loss of $5 million.

The next year, adapting to other realities, Barnes got out of the steel-making business as well.

For many years, all of the cold-rolled strip steel used by Associated Spring had been made by its own mill in Forestville, which first went into operation in 1914 to provide the company with a reliable source of raw materials. As time went on, however, its expanding spring divisions around the country found other specialty suppliers, and by the 1980s well over three quarters of the mill's output was being sold to customers outside the company. Not only was the mill no longer vital to Barnes's own operations, but it found itself in competition with larger steel makers in the U.S. and abroad that had their own pouring and hot-rolling capacities. It would require a major investment just to stay in the game.

While company officials were contemplating their options, a woman dropped into the Bristol headquarters one day, quite unannounced. The receptionist called upstairs, Wally Barnes remembers, and he asked what the woman wanted. After a pause came the reply: "She wants to buy the steel mill!" Said Wally, "Well, send her up!"

The visitor turned out to be Viola Hallman, the granddaughter of the

A Windsor Airmotive welder works inside a jet engine housing, one of thousands of components that the company overhauls for airlines and military clients every year.

WALLY BARNES

As a teenager, Wally Barnes used to hang around the Bristol airport, where he first fell in love with airplanes and learned how to fly. Today, at "Sky Bight," his modern home above Bristol, he can roll his twin Piper Aztec out of the garage, take off from his own airstrip and fly wherever he wants to go.

Often it's to Washington, D.C., for the weekend to be with Barbara Franklin, his wife, who runs a management consulting firm in the capital. Sometimes it's a special trip, to go canoeing in Canada, or to take a couple of his grandchildren to Newfoundland and Greenland so they can trace the route of America's Viking discoverers first hand. Says Barnes Vice President John Besser, a frequent companion on his North Country jaunts: "Flying is in Wally's blood. He loves any kind of adventure, and in tough situations he stays calm. There's no one I'd rather be stuck in the wilderness with."

Named for his great-grandfather, whom he admires as an adventurer and entrepreneur, Wallace Barnes took his love of flying into the U.S. Army Air Corps as an aviation cadet in World War II, graduated from Williams with honors in economics and from Yale Law School as a member of the law review. While still in college, he started his own charter airline, Nutmeg Air Transport, and later worked for Northeast Airlines, a commercial carrier, before deciding to put his law degree to use.

Wally soon tried his wings in politics, another of his loves.

While working as a partner in a Bristol law firm, he served as State Senator from his home district in 1958-1962 and again in 1966-1970, when he worked on court reform and environmental issues and was elected Senate Minority Leader. In 1970, he ran in the Republican gubernatorial primary against Thomas Meskill, who went on to become Governor of Connecticut.

An officer of the family company for 34 years, the last 14 as Chairman and CEO, Wally Barnes has found time to head everything from the Bristol Boys' Club to the University of Hartford's Board of Regents, as well as sitting on other corporate boards (including Aetna Life & Casualty, where he met another director—Barbara Franklin—and asked her to marry him).

Colleagues agree that Wally has an amiable air, but that he is no pushover when it comes to business. "He likes things to be done on time, and he likes them done right," says a member of the Barnes management team. "He can walk softly, but he can also carry a big stick. At the same time he's sympathetic, approachable; he supports and compliments. His greatest trademark is awareness. He's willing to try new things."

Perhaps most telling are the reactions of those who work on the production lines. Says one executive: "In some factories all you see is sullen faces. Not so here. And when Wally comes out to vis-

it a plant, it's a real happening. People on the floor call out, 'Hey, Wally, how are you?' How many CEO's can you say that about?

"He has a passion for the business, a passion for the parts, a passion for the people. People like to work for this company, and I think you've got to attribute a lot of that to Wally Barnes."

Wally Barnes as a budding pilot (top), and with wife Barbara Franklin near the air strip of their Bristol home.

founder of a German steel firm named Theis, and currently its Chairman and CEO. "She was a very determined lady," her host recalls. "She said she wanted to expand into the United States, either by making an acquisition or a joint venture or starting her own U.S. company. She

Jim Weidner packs die springs in the Corry, Pa. headquarters of Associated Spring's Raymond and SPEC distribution business, which ships over 60 million items a year.

said Theis had decided to come here, one way or another. To make a long story short, within a week we had the framework of a deal."

Once more a business, as well as a human, decision had to be made. "It was traumatic, like selling one of your children," says Wally. "This was the Wallace Barnes Steel Division, a name that had been known forever around Bristol. It wasn't easy."

He and other managers met with the workers at Forestville; they explained that the company felt the move was not only good for Barnes Group but for the employees themselves, that it would make everyone's future more secure. (By and large, it has. Except for Rich Glover, the new general manager that Theis appointed, and a few veterans who took early retirement, the work force has remained much the same.)

Meanwhile, Barnes was adding a fourth unit to its Aerospace Group. The new arrival was Jet Die & Engineering of Lansing, Michigan, a manufacturer of hot-formed components made from titanium and other lightweight "superalloys" with 112 employees and sales of $11 million a year. Skilled in shaping jet engine parts, airframes, struts, flaps and the like, Jet Die served General Electric and other aircraft engine manufacturers as well as marine and industrial users; a preponderance of its sales related to defense. The company was bought from Robert Soltow, its sole owner, for $15 million.

To manage its growing air arm,

Barnes had been looking around for an experienced hand. The company found the answer in Alex Jackson, President of Kelsey-Hayes's aerospace divisions in Michigan, who was named Barnes's Group Vice President for Aerospace Components the following year.

At the same time, new moves were being planned in Associated Spring, where the company's earlier contacts with Japan's NHK Spring Co. were starting to pay off. Among NHK's largest customers were Japanese automakers like Mazda, Nissan, Subaru, Toyota and Honda, which were establishing "transplant" factories in the United States to assemble cars for their growing American markets. To supply springs for those cars, NHK approached Barnes with the idea of a collaboration on U.S. soil. The result was the formation of NASCO, a $17 million joint venture between the two companies. Ground was broken for a new 60,000-square-foot plant for NASCO in Bowling Green, Kentucky, where some 50 workers would turn out coil suspension

THE BARNES AIR FORCE

Largely through Wally Barnes's personal love of flying, Barnes got into the use of its own aircraft early on. Beginning in the late 1950s, Wally himself flew executives to the company's far-flung plants in his four-seat Piper Apache, cutting a complex chore on commercial carriers to a day's round trip. When the convenience and speed proved of value, the company hired a pilot, Dick Kyte, to take over the task. Such flights not only made it easier for managers to keep in personal touch with their divisions but emboldened the company to expand to other locations out of easy airline range.

During the 1960s and 1970s the company used larger and faster aircraft, including twin-engined Beechcraft and Learjets, both around the U.S. and abroad. To help its newly acquired European operations learn from each other, Wally and Dick devised an aerial circus they dubbed "Operation Merry-Go-Round," in which the company plane shuttled technical personnel from one plant to the next in Sweden, England, Germany and The Netherlands; the plane dropped them off for two days so they could study their counterparts' operations, then returned to take them home. The exchange of ideas was such a success that the company staged other "merry-go-rounds" among its plants around the United States.

Today the company operates a twin-jet, seven-passenger Cessna Citation, which through careful scheduling it keeps busy five days a week, and occasionally on weekends as well. Pictured here with their aircraft, from left, are Royal Griffin, the current Manager of Flight Operations; Susan Chambers and John Moynihan, Aircraft Captains; and Robert Zabel, Aircraft Maintenance Supervisor. Together with their predecessors, they have compiled an award-winning safety record of more than 23,000 hours in the air over the course of the last three decades.

springs, using the latest Japanese methods of computerized, automated technology and quality controls. Under a technical assistance agreement, NHK also agreed to help Associated with a $7 million modernization of its valve-spring plants in Saline, Michigan, and Burlington, Ontario. The move not only improved the company's ability to supply valve springs to American automobile manufacturers, its traditional market, but to the new Japanese transplants as well.

In late 1987 the company had an experience it had not had before, and one that it hopes not to have again.

Barnes Group executives and directors were well aware of the financial climate of the 1980s, particularly the constant threat of corporate takeovers, which were then reaching a frenzied peak. Even the Barnes family's sizeable block of common stock, which amounted to some 35 percent of outstanding shares, was not an adequate defense.

Believing that the current price of Barnes Group stock did not reflect the true value of the company's business, assets and prospects, the Board had authorized the company to purchase up to 1.1 million shares. To help fund the purchases, an offering of $21 million of convertible preferred stock was to be sold to a friendly lender, the General Electric Credit Corporation.

One day before the Board was to finalize the plan, Barnes executives — in a letter delivered by ordinary mail — received the news they dreaded most: an outsider wanted to buy the company. He indicated that he already had a substantial stockholding in Barnes Group, and suggested the possibility of buying all of the company's stock at some price above $40 per share.

The overture from "Mr. X" (the company has agreed not to reveal his name) not only confirmed earlier fears. It also raised the specter that, when the news got out, the company might be put "in play" among a pack of voracious corporate raiders and Wall Street arbitrageurs. By the time it was all over, as other takeovers had all too clearly illustrated, Barnes Group could be either dismembered or dead.

A special meeting of the Board was called over the weekend in New York City. With the help of the company's investment bankers, Brown Brothers Harriman, and Skadden, Arps, Slate, Meagher & Flom, a New York law firm that specialized in takeovers, it was decided to go ahead with the stock-purchase program, consummate the GE deal and politely inform Mr. X that "now would be a most inopportune time to consider the sale of the company."

A week later, in a formal press release, Barnes Group announced that it had bought back the "interested party's" block of 308,300 shares on the New York Stock Exchange. (Almost two years later, the company repurchased its convertible preferred stock from General Electric Credit for $21.8 million.)

The takeover threat did not succeed, but the very idea of an outsider trying to steal their company was so repugnant to Barnes officials that it accomplished something else. "It concentrated our minds," says Stan Wells, forcing the company to think about the future in more creative ways.

Should another ogre appear on the scene, Barnes Group did not want to be put in the position of calling out like a damsel in distress, as other corporations had been forced to do. A sounder long-term strategy, it seemed, would be to have a larger percentage of its stock in friendly hands. A decision was made to encourage greater employee ownership by making an already generous stock-purchasing program even more attractive than it was.

Under its new Guaranteed Stock Plan, believed to be virtually unique at the time, Barnes in 1988 made it possible for employees to put aside up to 10 percent of their base pay through automatic payroll deductions. The company would then match those funds on the basis of 50 cents to the dollar, up to 6 percent of a worker's pay, and use the total to purchase Barnes Group common stock.

What was really innovative, however, was that the plan eliminated risk. It guaranteed that if Barnes stock had not done as well as the yield on two-year U.S. Treasury Notes by the time an employee was ready to withdraw his holdings, the company would make up the difference (on the amount represented by the employee's own savings, not on the company's matching funds). Since 1963, when Barnes stock was first offered on the New York Stock Exchange, it had averaged a compound growth of 11 percent a

Workers at Jet Die's facility in Lansing, Michigan, are experts in fabricating titanium and other advanced materials into parts for the aerospace industry. Here Sandra Welton assembles a strut for an F110 engine used in fighter aircraft.

year. All in all, an employee investor couldn't lose, and, if history were any indication, neither would the company.

The result was gratifying, even astonishing. In little more than a year, employee participation had grown to 76 percent. By mid-1991, the new guar-

Jet Die craftsman Ray Spitzley installs an assembly detail on a side panel used in several new-generation commercial jet engines.

anteed stock plan, which had become a leveraged ESOP, owned 17 percent of the outstanding common stock. Combined with an older stock purchasing plan and executive stock options, Barnes people now owned some 20 percent of the company for which they worked.

Moreover, that figure gave every indication of growing by 1 to 2 percentage points a year. The implication was evident. As Barnes family heirs became more numerous and more dispersed—there were already 50 or more, living around the country—and as some of them might be tempted to sell their stock in order to pursue other priorities, employee ownership could gradually take the place of a reduction in Barnes ownership.

Thus the old family company could

undergo a natural transition over a period of time, and one day might be controlled by a new, extended "family"—one, moreover, whose members were deeply involved in the company day by day. Wally and Hap Barnes had long been sold on the idea that if employees had a real stake in the company they would be better workers. The power of employee ownership was an idea whose time had come.

A new perspective was reflected at the company's annual employee meetings. "People used to say, 'Why did you do so-and-so?'," an executive noted. "Now it's 'Why did we do that?'" Adds a Barnes worker: "You can bet I watch the papers to see how my stock is doing. After all, it's not just my company. It's my money."

A corporate milestone of a more immediate kind was passed in 1989, when Barnes Group became a $500 million company, posting sales of $511,221,000.

By now Bowman had established itself as the company's biggest and most profitable business, rising from $18 million in sales by some 400 agents, when it was acquired in 1964, to sales of $231 million by some 900 agents—and income of more than $29 million—in 1989. Under its new Group Vice President, John Knapp (who had been President of ITT's Phillips Drill Division, a multinational operation headquartered in Indiana), Bowman had been growing at a compounded annual rate of 7 or 8 percent for several years. With its warehouses around the United States and Canada, and its van-distribution companies in England and France, it could boast of being "the world's largest direct-to-user distributor of repair and maintenance products."

Bowman celebrated its status by breaking ground for a new $2.5 million master warehouse in Elizabethtown, Kentucky, from which its regional distribution centers could draw products from stock, by computer linkup, in order to meet local customer demand. The division also expanded its Rockford, Illinois, warehouse, moved from Union, New Jersey, to larger new quarters in nearby Edison, and laid plans to expand its Norcross, Georgia, center. At the same time plans were made to close its facilities in Columbus, Ohio, and Colonial Heights, Virginia, which were no longer needed in the overall distribution scheme.

The same year marked the addition of a fifth unit to Barnes's Aerospace Group. The company acquired a majority of the assets of Flameco Engineering Inc. of Ogden, Utah, a privately-owned manufacturer of advanced components for aircraft engines and airframes with some 200 employees and two plants totaling 150,000 square feet. The $12 million transaction represented new life for Flameco, which had been faltering financially. Added to Jet Die, it meant more chances for Barnes Group to acquire new skills in the super-plastic forming and diffusion bonding of high-temperature alloys into precision parts.

As Barnes Group rounded the turn into the 1990s, Wallace Barnes announced that it was time for him to step down as Chief Executive Officer when he reached the age of 65. At the company's annual meeting in the spring of 1991, the Board elected William R. Fenoglio as CEO; Wally stayed on as Chairman of the Board (by company policy, which allows no directors 70 or older on its board, he would have to resign that post as well in 1996).

"Some people seem concerned that this is the first time in the company's history without a Barnes at the helm," he says. "I don't see it that way. I've been around long enough; it's just not appropriate for someone to be exercising authority over a living, vital organization any longer than that. Besides, the cast of characters really isn't going to change. Neither are the values that have driven the company for 134 years.

"At the same time, being the best at what we do will not be enough. We must continue to analyze where our skills fit in the overall competitive picture, and to continue to be flexible enough to change.

"So many of the companies I grew up with in this town—Ingraham, Sessions, Bristol Brass—to a kid they were immortal, but for one reason or another were taken over or just disappeared. How could those enormous buildings just go away? I don't want that to happen to us—I want this company to *survive*. And in the hands of Bill Fenoglio and our other professional managers, I have every confidence it will."

George Castle, engineering supervisor at Windsor Manufacturing, checks tooling drawings being produced by computer-aided design.

CHAPTER SIX

SHAPING THE FUTURE

A worker at Windsor Airmotive refurbishes a turbine exhaust part for a Boeing 747.

*What we need to address — what American
industry needs to address — is how to unlock the creative
capacities of all our people.*

— BILL FENOGLIO

F our years ago, Barnes Group sum-
marized its longstanding beliefs
in a "Guiding Philosophy," a set of
principles intended to serve as guidelines
for all its employees, from top managers
to hourly workers, and to tie its diverse
businesses together in a common strategy for success. In more than one way, it is
an extraordinary document. Bowman's
John Knapp describes it as "the glue that
holds the whole thing together."

At first glance, the statements (see
Appendices) might appear to be a corporate declaration of faith in Motherhood,
Baseball and the Bottom Line. Behind the
carefully chosen words, however, lie some
basic precepts of survival, as explained by
one of their principal authors, Wally Barnes:

WE EXIST TO SERVE OUR CUSTOMERS

"Unlike many companies, we don't
make an end product that consumers buy.
We make the bits and pieces and gadgets
that go into our customers' end products.
That's why we are more service businesses
than anything else.

"It's astonishing in the business
world how easy it is to fall in love with your
product, and all of a sudden you wake up
one day and nobody wants it any more.
How can this awful thing happen? You're
devastated. And you may very well be out
of business, too.

"At Barnes, we make a part today,
and then the product we're making it for
goes out of fashion. Look at our major
users of springs that have blossomed and
died over the years: wind-up clocks, mechanical comptometers, old-fashioned
adding machines. We used to make
springs by the skillions for them, but
those kinds of products just aren't around
anymore; they've been replaced.

*"It's astonishing how easy it
is to fall in love with your
product, and all of a sudden nobody
wants it any more."*

▼

WALLY BARNES
Chairman, Barnes Group

"So the marketplace forces us constantly to renew. It's the only way we have survived for more than a century. Indeed, it's the only way we can survive. At the end of the day what counts is what the customer wants, because it's the customer who pays the rent."

WE MUST FOCUS ON THOSE CUSTOMERS WHO RECOGNIZE AND REWARD SUPERIOR QUALITY AND SERVICE

"There are many manufacturers in the United States, but most of them don't make precision products, what we call 'critical parts.'

"We could make ordinary bed springs, for example, but upholstery manufacturers aren't interested in rewarding superior quality and service; a lot of people can make bed springs—they're not very complicated—so the manufacturers tend to buy purely by price. They don't need the kind of quality and service that we're geared up to supply, which is an expensive operation involving considerable technical overhead.

"Barnes has to keep sharpening its focus on the high end of the technological scale, in all of the businesses we serve. We have to walk away from the losers, and we have to charge the winners what they're worth. There's nothing wrong with charging what the market will bear—that's the way good companies operate. If a customer is willing to pay your price, then you're providing a degree of quality and service that someone else isn't.

"Having done that, however, and gained some experience with a particular job, you have to improve your production techniques so you can reduce the price. You can't stick to a dollar sign; you're just holding up an umbrella under which a lot of your competitors will crawl. So, after six months or so, without being asked, you go to the customer and say 'Hey, good news! We've had a better experience with your product than we thought; we've developed some new techniques, and we're going to give you a 10 percent cut in price.' There's nothing that pleases a customer more.

"That's where many of our Bowman agents are so good. They're face to face with their customers almost every day. They know whether a customer is pleased, or not pleased, or doesn't care. They know what price a customer is willing to pay, and when to reduce it. And if there's no way they can please a customer, they say OK, we can't serve you anymore. They walk away from him and go somewhere else.

"Sharpening the focus not only means getting better at what you do. It also means turning away business when that business doesn't make sense."

WE MUST FOCUS ON MANUFACTURING AND DISTRIBUTING PRODUCTS AND SERVICES WHERE WE HAVE, OR CAN GAIN, A COMPETITIVE ADVANTAGE

GOOD CITIZENS

"**W**e are a responsible corporate citizen [in the] communities in which we operate."

To many employees of Barnes Group, those words from the company's Guiding Philosophy are not empty ones; they are borne out in acts of compassion every day of the year. In towns where they live, uncounted individuals are involved in United Way campaigns, Boy and Girl Scout activities, Little Leagues, foster parenting, literacy tutoring, aid for handicapped persons, emergency shelters, hospitals, bloodmobiles.

One person who cares is Dick Lee, a shipper at Associated Spring's Raymond division in Corry, Pennsylvania, who for years has renovated or built homes for the homeless and disadvantaged through his organization "Carpenters for Christ." With the help of other employees like Dan McEldowney and Troy Nichols, Lee spends from 10 to 30 hours a week on projects that may mean reroofing a home for a destitute widow or adding a downstairs bedroom and bath for a family with a paralyzed child. A small wood-pallet business in Lee's workshop provides much of the funding. The Barnes Group Foundation has helped out with a $1,000 Volunteer Action Award, one of many that it distributes annually to worthy efforts around the country in which employees are actively involved.

For others, the young are a special concern. In Bristol, for example, some 70 employees help children from troubled homes who attend the Edgewood elementary school. Aided by an annual Barnes Group Foundation grant that underwrites projects and books, volunteers like Vice President-Controller John Locher (picture) take time out to read to lower-grade children every Friday (other readers have included President Bill Fenoglio and Chairman Wally Barnes). Additional "mentors" meet once a week with individual students they have adopted as young friends, playing games, helping with new activities, building confidence simply by being a companion who is willing to listen and care. Grace Sciarretta, a Corporate Office secretary, says her first-grade child was "just happy to find someone who likes to draw with her," a rewarding enough reason to keep coming back. Adds Carol Bernarduci, a secretary at Associated Spring, of her nine-year-old: "We may never see the overall results, but I hope that something I have done at this critical point will have significance later in that child's life."

In Saline and Gardena, employees have rallied to assist needy families at Christmas. In Cleveland, Bowman has raised funds to fight epilepsy. In England, Motalink workers have donated television sets to a local home for children with handicaps. And the list goes on.

Not a little of the spirit stems from Barnes family members themselves. For well over a century their initiative and support for a wide range of efforts in Bristol—youth clubs, cultural programs, a modern 250-bed hospital, nature preserves for environmental education—have helped to make their own home town a better place. Over the last 45 years the family has broadened its focus to include all of Connecticut. Today the Barnes Foundation supports scores of special projects, from drug education to opera appreciation, that provide new horizons for young people around the state.

"That means, basically, that we have to concentrate on products that others can't make at a profit, or that they can't make as well.

"Automobile valve springs are a classic example. If a valve spring breaks, the engine is destroyed, so the quality parameters are very high. We have developed a solid niche in that market because we can make a consistently high-quality spring at a competitive price—better than anyone else.

"That's the kind of product that we should focus on, not on something that anyone can make, like the little spring in a retractable ball-point pen. Unlike a valve spring, it's not very demanding, and when it breaks, well, you just throw the pen away. There's not a lot of expertise or close-tolerance work in that.

"We put a plant in Puerto Rico more than 30 years ago to make those kinds of springs because we thought we were losing the business, but we couldn't compete with mass manufacturers because the main criterion was price. We got driven right out of the market.

"What we should look for are new uses for the kind of high-strength, high-tech, high-precision products in which we excel."

PEOPLE ARE OUR
MOST IMPORTANT RESOURCE

"Our business is essentially a job-shop business. It's highly diverse, because we're turning out a lot of bits and pieces for a lot of customers.

"In that kind of business individual creativity is critical. Each order that comes in has different characteristics. Some human being has to respond to the problem in an intelligent, innovative way—he or she has to treat it as an individual challenge, to get into it with a sense of excitement. And if it's a reorder on a familiar product, then it's important to figure out how to make it, or deliver it, in a better and less costly way."

OUR VENDORS
ARE BUSINESS PARTNERS

"We're not interested solely in buying on the lowest price basis from the people who supply us with our raw mate-

"If we could get more people turned on, we could make some dramatic improvements."

▼

BILL FENOGLIO
President and CEO, Barnes Group

rials or distribution products. We're interested in long-term relationships with the kind of vendors who can help us attain a competitive edge.

"We go out of our way to have meetings with our vendors, to bring them into our plants, to explain our quality requirements to them, to work with them toward common goals.

"We like to be able to rely on our suppliers, just as we like our customers to be able to rely on us."

WE ARE A RESPONSIBLE CORPORATE CITIZEN

"In human terms, that means being responsive to the needs of the communities in which we operate—not only supporting worthy causes as a company but encouraging our employees to do so as individuals.

"In business terms, it means being honest—conducting your business in accordance with the highest ethical standards, as you would your personal life. It's not only a moral obligation, but a matter of sound business practice as well.

"We don't believe in cheating on quality, or allowing defective products to be shipped, or taking kickbacks from customers, or making side deals with vendors. Companies that operate that way in the long run won't only be wrong. Ultimately they won't succeed.

"There are some people, I guess, who think this kind of thing is not all that important. We think it is."

SUPERIOR FINANCIAL RESULTS WILL FOLLOW AS A NATURAL OUTCOME

"Typically, a business will say we have a goal of such-and-such a return on capital. We have backed off from that kind of definitive statement.

"We simply say, as an article of faith, that if we do the things we say we're going to do, then superior—not just good—financial results will follow as a matter of course."

One way to accomplish these goals, Wally Barnes explains, is to give each unit in a diverse company like Barnes Group more autonomy to act on its own, which cuts down on its response

"If we target one or two specific industries a year, we'll enhance our penetration in those fields."

▼

JOHN KNAPP
Group Vice President, Bowman Distribution

time in terms of design, price quotation and production. Response time, he points out, is becoming every bit as important as price and quality as a competitive tool, especially in a service business like Barnes.

"Each of our units must be able to respond to its customers' needs—and quickly," he says. "The only way that can happen is for them to perceive their unit almost as if it were their own company, and not be hampered by a bureaucratic structure above.

"We are learning a lot from the Japanese. They invented a whole new system of manufacturing by teamwork, and we are adapting it in some of our plants. Beyond that, they are unusually responsive to the marketplace, constantly making the kinds of refinements that their customers want. They don't sit in an ivory tower and decide what to give people. They listen to what people say."

Bill Fenoglio and others of the management team agree. After all, they helped to formulate the philosophy, and in the future they will have to carry it out. Here are some of the criteria Fenoglio believes to be vital in shaping the future of the company:

ON PRODUCT FOCUS: "We must focus on products with good margins, and we must do a better job of controlling costs. I know it's sometimes difficult to give up less profitable lines that we've made for many years. But that's exactly what we have to do.

"I really don't believe in miracles in

"I want a person to be able
to walk into the manager's office
and say, 'I've got an idea.'
And for the manager to reply,
'Go ahead and try it.'"

▼

ALEX JACKSON
Group Vice President, Barnes Aerospace

business. With the economic uncertainties of the global marketplace, I don't expect great gains in sales. It's earnings we must improve. That's our challenge for the 1990s and beyond."

ON PROFITABILITY: "Right now our financial performance is middle of the road. I'd like to see us get into the top 25 percent of companies in profitability. There's no reason why Barnes Group can't double its current return on sales, and increase its return on equity by a third or more. We see improvements in many of our operations, but we still have a way to go."

ON PRODUCTIVITY: " 'Continuous improvement' isn't just a buzzword. It really means being better next week than this week, better next year than this year, and that's not always easy to do. It's like telling Ted Williams, when he batted .406 one season, that he has to hit .410 or better the next. You have to measure yourself constantly against what you've done. Even more important, you have to measure yourself against the benchmark companies of the world in the kind of business you're in.

"You can be getting better but losing the race, simply because you're not improving as fast as your competition. In valve springs, for example, we benchmark ourselves against NHK in Japan. We visit their factories, we send managers and hourly workers there to find out what they do and how. We want to see what kind of an operation it is that produces suggestions at a rate of hundreds per employee per year, where in our own divisions we might struggle to get a half dozen.

"That's one of the reasons Japan is leading the world in manufacturing. When Japanese employees arrive at the plant in the morning, they're thinking 'How can I do my job better?' If we're going to stay in the race, we'd better think about that."

ON EMPLOYEE INVOLVEMENT: "What we need to address—what American industry needs to address—is how to unlock the intellectual and creative capacities of all our people. There are still a lot of employees who check their brains at the door when they come to work; they stand in front of a machine or sit at a desk and think about something else. But when they're not at work, those same employees run school boards, United Way agencies, church fund raisers. Somehow we have to unlock that talent, and direct it to the tasks at hand. Right now we're running on four out of eight cylinders. If we could get more people turned on, running on all cylinders, we could make some dramatic improvements.

"Sometimes, unfortunately, it takes fear to get people's attention. Some of the most effective turnarounds I've seen in 30 years in business are when companies have come very close to the edge, when everyone suddenly realized that they were all in the same boat and they'd bet-

"What you have to do is constantly take little incremental steps—there may be a thousand of them—toward greater efficiency."

▼

TED MARTIN
Group Vice President, Associated Spring

A BETTER WAY

Around Barnes Group, "continuous improvement" is the name of the game—searching for new ways to deliver a better product at a lower cost. And, as the company has discovered, the best ideas usually come not from consulting engineers or other outside experts, but from workers who deal with the problems every day.

Employee suggestion plans, of course, are nothing new. Associated Spring has had an awards program for more than 30 years. Divisions of the Aerospace Group have developed their own systems for eliciting and rewarding ideas, from taking the winners out to dinner to sharing a percentage of the money saved.

Bowman Distribution has staged an intensive idea search nicknamed "Click!" Out of submissions by 515 employees, encouraged to work in teams, it garnered 140 improvements worthy of putting into effect—at a savings to the company of a half million dollars a year. One bright idea (and to the average package recipient, perhaps long overdue) was worth an estimated $70,000 alone: Get rid of messy styrofoam "peanuts" to cushion parts shipments and buy shredders to recycle used paper and cardboard instead.

A productivity breakthrough of 20 or 25 percent is rare; most divisions are happy to settle for ideas that can result in a 1 or 2 percent gain. A concerted push, however, can sometimes bring about dramatic results.

Such was the case with the newly acquired Flameco Division in Ogden, Utah, which had won a key contract with Kelly Air Force Base in Texas to manufacture 12,000 complex nozzle parts used in the afterburners of F-15 and F-16 fighters. The program called for 14 man hours per part, but actual costs were running over 50 man hours, threatening a financial disaster.

Flameco set up a team of 10 separate "cells," each responsible for its own area—welding, machining, chemical processing,

Flameco's Robin Whitehouse and Sherry Sanders, precision-machining a titanium part.

hand finishing, flame spraying—and each working closely with other cells in a rigorous system of statistical process control. The task of reducing scrap and rework was assigned to workers closest to the problems, who came up with a host of suggestions for improvements. Over the course of a year, man hours per part gradually came down to 28, then to less than 11—providing the company with the confidence to bid on, and win, a $21 million contract for an additional 21,000 parts.

The team celebrated with a picnic, then buckled down again, this time to reduce production time to 8 man hours per part. Says Flameco president Stuart Kale: "With that kind of pride and commitment, they may well do even better."

ter row together or sink. We had something like that happen four or five years ago in Ann Arbor. It was the union that said: 'Look, we know if we all keep going along this way, we're going to lose this plant, and our jobs; we're willing to make compromises to help keep this business secure.' We renegotiated a contract, and we invested in a whole new automated plant in Saline. That's the kind of turnaround I'm talking about.

"But we can make a lot of progress without that kind of last-ditch effort. It's a good sign that people are asking questions, wanting to know why things are being done. They want to know where their company is going, what it stands for, what it means to belong to Barnes Group. You read a lot of articles these days about loss of loyalty, that it doesn't mean anything anymore. I think that's the fault of management, not the workers. Most people want to belong to an organization, to contribute and to be proud of who they work for. The challenge to all managers is to maximize the contribution of their people — to get them involved in making their business stronger."

ON NEW MARKET OPPORTUNITIES: "One of our key opportunities for the future is in distribution, both in maintenance products and in springs, especially in SPEC and replacement die springs, where the margins are particularly good.

"At Bowman we do a very good business, but we only have something like 1 percent of the U.S. maintenance and repair market. Rather than running around trying to buy new companies, our number one priority should be to get more of that other 99 percent. The same priority applies at Associated Spring and Aerospace—to get a larger share of the huge market that we have right under our noses.

"Bowman in particular has some potentially excellent opportunities in so-called integrated maintenance, where customers are looking for people who will not only sell them products but will manage their tool cribs, be their in-house maintenance material experts.

"One of these days I'd like to see a Bowman Europe, a clone of Bowman North America. With the 'new Europe' developing, there's no reason we shouldn't be the leading supplier of maintenance and repair products there. The same thing applies to the distribution of our springs.

"We're going to have a stronger international focus in the next 10 years, but we won't rush into unprofitable situations. We'll pursue opportunities in Europe if they are as good or better than we can accomplish here in the U.S. We must take what we have to offer to where the markets are. One of the most effective ways may be to form affiliations or joint ventures with European counterparts, and that goes for Asia, too.

"In Aerospace, we have a unique product niche with Jet Die and Flameco. How do we drive that worldwide? How do we become a global leader in the repair of jet-engine components? We've already expanded Windsor Airmotive into the Far East in Singapore, but Europe is waiting."

Bill Fenoglio's views are bolstered by others directly concerned with Barnes Group divisions and their employees.

Says John Knapp, Group Vice President of Bowman Distribution: "We can't be all things to all people; we have to be more selective, to focus on target areas as a way of increasing sales. We've done that at Bowman with trucking fleets, and our sales went up 20 or 25 percent. We've been doing it with the construction industry, the waste management industry, the food industry, also with good results. If we target one or two specific industries a year over the next decade, we'll enhance our penetration in those fields."

Says Alex Jackson, Group Vice President of Aerospace: "When we buy a new piece of equipment, I want the person who is actually going to run it to be a part of the acquisition study, to have a say in what that machine should be.

"I also want a person who is making a part to be able to walk into the general manager's office and say, 'I've got an idea that could take an hour out of that part.' And for the manager to reply, 'Go ahead and try it.' If the idea fails—some ideas do—I don't want the guy to have his head taken off; I'd like to see everyone have a meeting and go through the whole thing and see what happened, how

it might lead to a better solution. If the idea works, then I want the person to feel he really contributed something, and for everybody to know that he did.

"In some of our plants, we have a cash-for-ideas plan, where a person gets a bonus based on the potential savings in implementing an idea over a period of time. I have no reason to change that. The only danger with a payment plan, however, is that people might tend to hide a good idea until they felt the price was right, or that you might be singling out somebody who did half what another person did. The approach I prefer is to recognize a team that has made a contribution, with an announcement, a flyer, then have the boss take the members of the team and their spouses out to dinner. That means a lot."

Says Donald Snowberger, Vice President for Human Resources: "Each of our units has its own management style, its own system of rewards. There's no one way to do things. In many of our management meetings we are looking for different ways to accomplish our goal.

"We have many different cultures within the company, from the hierarchical type where the boss says, 'Do it this way,' to participative types where the manager sits down with a group and says, 'Here's the problem and the goal; what's the best way to achieve it?' Both those systems can work, but they need to be constantly examined, and constantly fine-tuned, because circumstances change and people change.

"We've made it clear that the company would prefer a more participative style, that the days of the autocrat are over. But of all the companies I've worked for, the managers here have more power to run their segments of the business than any other. They aren't strapped by all sorts of corporate directives. They set the targets of what they're going to achieve. There's no one saying from above, 'You will make another 25 percent this year'—a figure that may have been inflated unrealistically because someone wants to show an upward line on a chart.

"**W**e've tried to put up a philosophical umbrella that says, 'We want you to be fair, we want you to be straight, we want you to be involved with your people, we want to get everybody into the game because that ties in with our philosophy of employee ownership.' How you actually get there is something else. We say, 'Do what you think is best for your operation, and if you need help it will be made available.'

"We've got a grand history as a company, but we're not invincible. There's no sense kidding anybody in this day and age. We have to be world-class and competitive; we have to be the best there is, because there'll always be somebody out there trying to eat our lunch. It's a dogfight, and there aren't any guarantees."

Other voices are being heard as Barnes moves into the 1990s, its 14th decade of corporate life.

The newest member of top management is Theodore Martin, an ex-Air Force pilot with 22 years of industrial experience before becoming Group Vice President of Associated Spring late last year.

Says Martin: "Change is inevitable—as they say in business, if you don't change you die. What we have to do is make people comfortable with change, before it becomes an issue. We have to get the most skilled people possible for the jobs we have available—whether they're from minority groups, whether they're women, I couldn't care less.

"In fact, with women becoming more than half the work force in America, we can't afford any longer to have a job that requires lifting 200 pounds; that just won't fly. We have to change the process so it's done automatically, by a machine instead of brute muscle, and we're smart enough to do that.

"If there are language problems in some of our plants, like employees who are mainly Spanish-speaking, we should provide some sort of language training. And it shouldn't be just a one-way thing so they learn better English; it should include a program so that English-speaking employees learn a little Spanish, too. That's only fair.

"You rarely hit a home run in our kind of business," Martin concludes. "What you have to do is constantly take little incremental steps—there may be a thousand of them—toward greater efficiency. Our people know their products very well, and they know their machines. But they have to feel that they're part of the decision-making process, that their contributions are valued, and will be recognized."

In the end, that simple human statement may say more than any corporate credo about what really makes the wheels go round. Bill Fenoglio sums it up: "Barnes is a family kind of company; indeed, that is its greatest strength. An overriding concern for people will continue to determine our course—and our survival—in the years ahead."

At NASCO's highly automated plant in Bowling Green, Kentucky, red-hot steel rods are coiled into automobile suspension springs for Honda, Toyota, Nissan and other Japanese "transplant" manufacturers in the U.S. A joint venture of Associated Spring and Yokohama's NHK Spring Company, NASCO is directed by a team of NHK experts who stress the Japanese concept of kaizen *("continuous improvement") in daily meetings among the company's 75 employees.*

APPENDICES

GUIDING PHILOSOPHY

Barnes Group is a diversified public company consisting of three separate businesses dedicated to providing superior quality products and services to selected industrial markets. We believe that:

WE EXIST TO SERVE OUR CUSTOMERS.

WE MUST FOCUS ON THOSE CUSTOMERS WHO RECOGNIZE AND REWARD SUPERIOR QUALITY AND SERVICE.

WE MUST FOCUS ON MANUFACTURING AND DISTRIBUTING PRODUCTS AND SERVICES WHERE WE HAVE, OR CAN GAIN, A COMPETITIVE ADVANTAGE.

PEOPLE ARE OUR MOST IMPORTANT RESOURCE. WE WILL FOSTER A DECENTRALIZED, ENTREPRENEURIAL ENVIRONMENT WHERE EACH PERSON IS RESPECTED AS AN IN-DIVIDUAL WHO CAN MAKE SIGNIFICANT CONTRIBUTIONS TO THE SUCCESS OF THE COMPANY. WE WILL PROVIDE AN ATMOSPHERE OF PARTICIPATION AND PARTNER-SHIP WHICH ENCOURAGES OPEN COMMUNICATION, INDIVIDUAL CREATIVITY, AND A CONTINUING SEARCH FOR BETTER WAYS TO CONDUCT OUR BUSINESS. WE EX-PECT SUPERIOR PERFORMANCE AND WILL PAY FOR IT.

OUR VENDORS ARE BUSINESS PARTNERS. WE INTEND TO DEVELOP LONG-TERM RELA-TIONSHIPS AT FAIR PRICES WITH VENDORS WHO HELP US ATTAIN COMPETITIVE ADVANTAGE THROUGH QUALITY, INNOVATION AND ON-TIME DELIVERY.

WE ARE A RESPONSIBLE CORPORATE CITIZEN. WE WILL CONDUCT OUR BUSINESS IN AC-CORD WITH THE HIGHEST ETHICAL STANDARDS, AND BE RESPONSIVE TO THE CONCERNS OF THE COUNTRIES AND COMMUNITIES IN WHICH WE OPERATE.

SUPERIOR FINANCIAL RESULTS WILL FOLLOW AS A NATURAL OUTCOME OF OUR EFFORTS.

OUR ACTIONS AS A CORPORATION WILL BE FULLY CONSISTENT WITH THESE BELIEFS, ENABLING BARNES GROUP AND ITS STOCKHOLDERS TO CONTINUE TO PROSPER IN AN EVER CHANGING WORLD.

Adopted by the Board of Directors,
February 20, 1987

Ford Motor Company	*Ford Q–1 Award*
Pratt & Whitney Canada, UTC	*Accredited Supplier Award*
Caterpillar	*Certified Supplier*
GE Aircraft Engine Business Group	*Supplier Excellence Award*
Bendix / Siemens	*Qualified Supplier*
Pratt & Whitney	*Quality Achievement Award*
Graco, Inc.	*Certified Supplier*
Textron Lycoming	*Designated Supplier Quality Program Accreditation*
GMC / Hydra-Matic	*Phase #1 Supplier Certification*
Eaton Power Distribution Division	*Certificate of Verification*
Eaton / Cutler-Hammer	*Quality First Award*
Ford Aerospace	*Team #1 Member*
Northern Telecom	*Certified Vendor*
Chrysler	*Pentastar Award*
Steelcase, Inc.	*Quality Excellence Award*
Navistar	*Certified Supplier*
Johnson Controls, Inc.	*Superior Award*
GM do Brasil	*Quality Award*
Garrett Turbine	*Preferred Supplier*
Western Gear	*Quality Supplier*
Motorola	*Excellence in Customer Service*
Hitachi	*Good Performance Award*
Kodak	*Certified Supplier*
General Motors of Canada	*Targets for Excellence-Quality*
Consolidated Diesel	*Vendor Certification Award*
IBM	*Zero Defects in Quality*
Mercedes	*Certified Supplier*
Webster City Products	*Supplier of the Year*
Texas Instruments	*100% Rating*
Western Electric Corporation	*Outstanding Award*
Allison Gas Turbine	*100% Quality Rating*
GM de Mexico	*Outstanding Supplier*
Square D	*Certified Supplier*
Robertshaw Controls	*Key to Quality Award*
Moog Automotive	*Certified Supplier*
Honeywell	*Certified Supplier*
Moto Honda	*Certified Supplier Award*
Andreas Stihl	*Quality Award*
AT&T	*Preferred II Supplier*
Control Data	*100% Quality Rating*

Over the years, divisions of Barnes Group have won scores of awards from customers for the quality of their products. Listed here are a few of the most recent awards.

1857 Wallace Barnes founds his own small company in Bristol, starts making springs for clocks and hoop skirts with E. L. Dunbar.

1893 Wallace Barnes dies, leaving his son Carlyle to manage the family's business affairs.

1913 Fuller F. Barnes, Carlyle's son, is made General Manager.

1914 Steel rolling mill is built in the Forestville section of Bristol.

1914-1918 World War I. Barnes makes ordnance parts for the Allies.

1921 Wallace Barnes Co., Ltd. established in Hamilton, Ontario.

1922 Barnes-Gibson-Raymond, Inc. founded in Detroit.

1923 BGR formed into the Associated Spring Corporation. Wallace Barnes Division purchases Dunbar Bros. Co.

1929 Acquisition of Cook Spring Co., Ann Arbor, Michigan.

1932 Depth of the Great Depression. Wages reduced at all plants.

1937 F. N. Manross & Sons purchased by Associated Spring.

1939-1945 World War II. Company wins 15 Army-Navy "E" awards.

1944 Raymond Merchandise Division started in Corry, Pennsylvania.

1946 Associated Spring stock is offered for sale over the counter.

1947 Ohio Division established in Dayton.

1949 Major addition to steel mill in Forestville.

1950 Milwaukee Division started in Wisconsin. Sales office opened in Cleveland. Pension plans established for employees.

1951 Carlyle F. ("Hap") Barnes made General Manager of Wallace Barnes Co. BGR Division moves to a new plant in Plymouth, Michigan.

1952 Acquisition of Seaboard Coil Spring Corp., Los Angeles.

1953 Annual sales pass $50 million. Hap Barnes becomes President.

1957 Company's 100th anniversary. Research and Development Center started in Bristol. New spring-making plant built in Quebec.

1959 ASC affiliates with Resortes Argentina S.A. Gibson Division moves to a new plant in Mattoon, Illinois.

1960 ASC Merchandise Division, begun as part of Raymond, is established on its own in Corry, Pennyslvania.

1961 ASC inaugurates an employee suggestion plan with cash awards ranging from $10 to $5,000 for cost-cutting ideas. ASC affiliates with Tempered Group, Ltd. of Sheffield, England.

1962 Acquisition of Westmetal Products Co., Los Angeles. ASC springs used in space suits for Astronaut John Glenn's flight, first to orbit Earth.

1963 Associated Spring is listed on the New York Stock Exchange.

1964 ASC purchases Bowman Products of Cleveland, national distributor of repair and replacement parts. Three companies acquired in Mexico. Hap Barnes elected Chairman and Chief Executive Officer; Wally Barnes becomes President and Chief Operating Officer. A Monthly Investment Plan permits employees to purchase company stock.

1965 Bowman opens new distribution centers in Georgia and New Jersey, establishes Bowman S.A. de C.V. in Mexico City.

1966 ASC acquires Tevema in The Netherlands, Broadbent & Co. in England. Plants are built in Chicago and North Carolina. ASC stock is split 3 for 2.

1967 Spirex Screw Co. opens a new plant in Akron, Ohio. Milwaukee Division moves to a new facility at Airport Industrial Park.

1968 Sales pass the $100 million mark. Acquisition of the Frank Holister Co. of Dallas, maker of concrete reinforcing and metal parts.

1969 Apollo 11, with ASC springs aboard, lands first man on the moon. Bowman opens a distribution center in Edmonton, Alberta.

1970 Construction starts on a $5 million factory building in Bristol. Associated Spring is listed on the London Stock Exchange.

1971 ASC acquires STECE AB of Sweden and Herbert Terry & Sons of England. Bowman builds a master warehouse in Elizabethtown, Kentucky, to serve nine regional distribution centers.

1973 Acquisition of Motalink Ltd. of England, Autoliaisons of France, Atlas Fastener of Cleveland. Bowman opens a new distribution center near Seattle, Washington.

1974 The company acquires Indap S.A., manufacturer of custom metal parts in São Paulo, Brazil.

1975 ASC establishes a scholarship program for employees' children. Bowman opens distribution centers in California and Alaska.

1976 Name changed from Associated Spring Corporation to Barnes Group Inc. Acquisition of Stumpp & Schuele of West Germany, Brazil and India. New spring plant opened in Dallas. Stock split 2 for 1.

1977 Wallace Barnes becomes Chairman of the Board and Chief Executive Officer; Carlyle Barnes elected Chairman of the Executive Committee; Jeremiah McQuillan becomes President. At a dinner in Bristol, 167 employees are honored for 3,140 years of service.

1978 Barnes Group acquires Globe Industries, Inc., distributor of do-it-yourself auto replacement parts and hardware. Highest award yet for an employee suggestion—$3,173 for improved tooling on a grinding operation—goes to Joseph Lasnier of Wallace Barnes Steel Division.

1979 Completion of new Barnes Group headquarters building in Bristol. Acquisition of Pioneer Products, Inc. of Mississippi and Chanenson Corp. of Illinois.

1980 Globe breaks ground for a distribution center in Gainesville, Georgia. New factory completed for Stumpp & Schuele in Brazil.

1981 Company enters aerospace field with the acquisition of Central Metal Products of East Windsor, Connecticut. New Bowman warehouse opens in New Brunswick, Canada. Associated Spring opens new plants in Ontario and

Singapore, buys Herckelbout-Dawson of France.

1982 Barnes Group reports a $2.7 million loss. Plymouth, Michigan, plant is closed. Windsor Manufacturing of Windsor, Connecticut, is acquired to form the new Aerospace Components group.

1983 Barnes reports a $2.6 million loss, closes three spring plants in North America. Divestitures in North America, Europe, and Latin America are completed.

1984 Profits at Associated Spring rebound to $15.7 million.

1985 Jeremiah McQuillan retires as President, is succeeded by William Fenoglio. Globe Distribution is sold. Bowman opens centers in Ontario and Georgia, installs a new testing laboratory and mainframe computer in Cleveland. Pioneer adds a distribution center in New Jersey.

1986 Acquisition of Jet Die & Engineering Inc. of Lansing, Michigan. NASCO, a joint venture with NHK Spring Co. of Japan, begins building a plant in Kentucky. Bristol steel mill is sold.

1987 Construction starts on a valve-spring plant in Saline, Michigan, to replace the Ann Arbor facility. Bowman opens a distribution center in Montreal. Barnes fends off a takeover threat by selling $21 million of stock to General Electric Credit Corporation.

1988 A Guaranteed Stock Plan is offered to employees.

1989 Annual sales exceed $500 million. Bowman breaks ground for a master warehouse in Elizabethtown, Kentucky, expands its Rockford, Illinois, warehouse, moves to larger quarters in New Jersey. Acquisition of Flameco Engineering Inc. of Ogden, Utah.

1990 Windsor Airmotive starts construction on a jet-engine overhaul facility in Singapore. NASCO doubles capacity, adding 60,000-sq.-ft. plant expansion and second automated coil suspension spring line.

1991 Wallace Barnes steps down as Chief Executive Officer and is succeeded by President William Fenoglio. Barnes continues as Chairman of the Board.

YEARS OF GROWTH

The company's performance since its shares were first offered on the New York Stock Exchange in 1963.

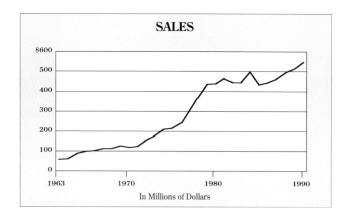

SALES

In Millions of Dollars

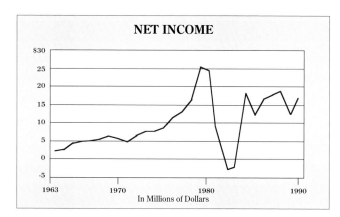

NET INCOME

In Millions of Dollars

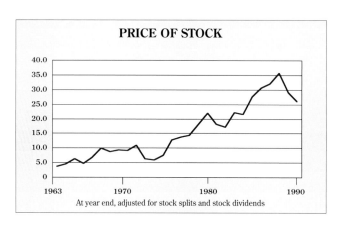

PRICE OF STOCK

At year end, adjusted for stock splits and stock dividends

BARNES GROUP INC.
Executive Office, Bristol, Connecticut

....

BOWMAN DISTRIBUTION

Group Headquarters:
Cleveland, Ohio

BOWMAN-U.S.

Headquarters:
Cleveland, Ohio

DISTRIBUTION CENTERS

Bakersfield, California
Norcross, Georgia
Rockford, Illinois
Elizabethtown, Kentucky
Edison, New Jersey
Arlington, Texas
Houston, Texas
Kent, Washington

OTHER DISTRIBUTION OPERATIONS

PIONEER
Meridian, Mississippi
Cerritos, California
Bensenville, Illinois
Mt. Laurel, New Jersey

BOWMAN-INTERNATIONAL

CANADA:
Concord, Ontario
Edmonton, Alberta
Moncton, New Brunswick
St. Laurent, Quebec

UNITED KINGDOM:
Motalink Ltd.,
Corsham, England

FRANCE:
Autoliaisons France S.A.,
Voisins Le Brettoneux

BARNES AEROSPACE

Group Headquarters:
Windsor, Connecticut

PRECISION MACHINING:

CENTRAL METAL PRODUCTS
East Windsor, Connecticut

WINDSOR MANUFACTURING
Windsor, Connecticut

ADVANCED FABRICATIONS:

FLAMECO
Ogden, Utah

JET DIE
Lansing, Michigan

OVERHAUL AND REPAIR:

WINDSOR AIRMOTIVE
East Granby, Connecticut
Republic of Singapore

ASSOCIATED SPRING

Group Headquarters:
Bristol, Connecticut

NORTH AMERICAN PLANTS

Gardena, California
Bristol, Connecticut
Saline, Michigan
Syracuse, New York
Arden, North Carolina
Dayton, Ohio
Burlington, Ontario
Corry, Pennsylvania
Memphis, Tennessee
Dallas, Texas
Milwaukee, Wisconsin

DISTRIBUTION OPERATIONS

ASSOCIATED SPRING - RAYMOND
Corry, Pennsylvania
Cerritos, California
Arlington, Texas

INTERNATIONAL

UNITED KINGDOM:
Associated Spring SPEC Ltd.,
Evesham, England
BRAZIL:
Stumpp & Schuele do Brazil,
Industria e
Comercio Limitada,
Campinas
MEXICO:
Resortes Mecanicos S.A.,
Mexico, D.F.
Resortes Industriales del
Norte S.A.,
Monterrey, N.L.
SINGAPORE:
Associated Spring-Asia
PTE Ltd.,
Republic of Singapore

DIRECTORS AND OFFICERS

BOARD OF DIRECTORS

Carlyle F. Barnes
Retired Senior Officer
of the Company

Thomas O. Barnes
President
The Olson Brothers Company
Plainville, Connecticut

Wallace Barnes
Chairman of the Board

William S. Bristow, Jr.
New England Regional
Sales Manager
Parcel Plus Inc.
Northampton, New Hampshire

Robert J. Callander†
President and Director
Chemical Banking Corp.
and Chemical Bank
New York, New York

George T. Carpenter
President
The S. Carpenter
Construction Company
Bristol, Connecticut

Donna R. Ecton
Former Senior Vice President
Nutri/System, Inc.
Willow Grove, Pennsylvania

William R. Fenoglio
President and Chief
Executive Officer

Marcel P. Joseph†
Chairman of the Board, Chief
Executive Officer and President
Augat Inc.
Mansfield, Massachusetts

Bernard N. Kelly*
Bernard Kelly & Associates
London, England

Richard K. LeBlond, II*
Senior Advisor and Retired
Vice Chairman and Director
Chemical Bank
New York, New York

Juan M. Steta
Partner
Santamarina y Steta,
Attorneys at Law
Mexico, D.F., Mexico

K. Grahame Walker
President, Chief Executive
Officer and Director
The Dexter Corporation
Windsor Locks, Connecticut

Boris Yavitz
Garrett Professor of
Public Policy and Business
Responsibility, and former Dean
Graduate School of Business
Columbia University
New York, New York

*retired 1991
† elected 1991

EXECUTIVE OFFICE

William R. Fenoglio
President and Chief
Executive Officer

A. Stanton Wells
Executive Vice
President - Finance

Richard D. Hines
Senior Vice President

John E. Besser
Vice President, General Counsel
and Secretary

George J. Crowley
Vice President and Treasurer

John J. Locher
Vice President and Controller

Robert F. O'Connor
Vice President - Corporate
Development and Planning

Donald E. Snowberger
Vice President -
Human Resources

Mary Louise Beardsley
Assistant General Counsel
and Assistant Secretary

Francis C. Boyle, Jr.
Assistant Controller

OPERATIONS

Theodore E. Martin
Group Vice President
Associated Spring

Alexander Jackson III
Group Vice President
Barnes Aerospace

John M. Knapp
Group Vice President
Bowman Distribution

Charles G. Rowley
Vice President
Associated Spring Operations

Adams, Lyman D. *The "Why and Wherefore" of the Associated Spring Corporation,* privately printed by the Davis Press, Inc. for Associated Spring Corporation, Bristol, Connecticut, 1953.

Associated Spring Corporation. *The How and Why of Associated Spring Corporation,* Bristol, Connecticut, 1971.

Bailey, Chris. *Two Hundred Years of American Clocks & Watches*, Prentice-Hall, Inc., Englewood Cliffs, New Jersey, 1975.

Barnes Group Inc. *Annual Reports* and other literature, various dates.

Beals, Carleton. *Our Yankee Heritage: The Making of Bristol*, Bristol Public Library Association, 1954.

The Bristol Press. Special Section: *Barnes Group Opens International Headquarters,* Bristol, Connecticut, July 19, 1979.

Clouette, Bruce and Matthew Roth. *Bristol, Connecticut: A Bicentennial History/1785-1985*, Bristol Public Library/Phoenix Publishing, Canaan, New Hampshire, 1984.

Fawcett, W. Peyton. *History of the Spring Industry,* Spring Manufacturers Institute, Wheeling, Illinois, 1983.

Grant, Ellsworth Strong. *Yankee Dreamers and Doers,* Pequot Press, Chester, Connecticut, 1973.

Hull, George W. *The Saga of the Barnes Family*, Connecticut Circle, undated.

Hull, Mr. and Mrs. George W. *Ten Generations of the Barn(e)s Family in Bristol, Connecticut*, privately printed by Fuller F. Barnes, 1946.

The Main Spring, published monthly by and for the employees of The Wallace Barnes Company, 1919-1921 issues.

The Mainspring, an external publication for industry readers, various issues, 1928-1968.

Osborn, Norris Galpin, ed. *History of Connecticut in Monographic Form, Volume IV*, The States History Company, New York, 1925.

Palmer, Brooks. *A Treasury of American Clocks*, The Macmillan Co., New York, 1967.

Peck, Epaphroditus. *History of Bristol, Connecticut*, The Lewis Street Bookshop, Hartford, Connecticut, 1932.

Wallace Barnes Company Division of Associated Spring Corporation. *"Springs Eternal": A Century of Fine Springmaking 1857-1957*, Bristol, Connecticut, 1957.

Acknowledgments and Credits

THE AUTHOR is grateful to the many people of Barnes Group who contributed to the making of this book, especially Wally Barnes, Chairman of the Board, who approved the project and helped greatly with the content, and Jack Sand, Director of Public Affairs, who provided invaluable guidance. Thanks are also due to Leonard Wolfe, design director Richard Warner, Alice Cooke, Candy Katsarakes and Ruth Wolfe for their high degree of professionalism in design and production.

OGDEN TANNER, the author, a freelance writer and editor, lives in New Canaan, Connecticut. A graduate of Princeton University, he worked as a reporter and feature writer for the San Francisco *Chronicle*, then for 22 years at Time Inc. in New York, where he was a senior editor of *Architectural Forum* magazine and Time-Life Books. He has written many books and articles on business, history, architecture, gardening, nature and the environment.

ILLUSTRATIONS

(BGA = Barnes Group Archives)

Cover and flyleaf: engravings from *Ten Generations of the Barn(e)s Family in Bristol, Connecticut,* privately printed by Fuller F. Barnes, 1946. **Page 2:** BGA, photo by Peter Maronn. **Page 4:** BGA. **Page 5:** courtesy American Clock and Watch Museum, Bristol, photo by Rick LaBranche. **Page 6:** BGA. **Page 7:** BGA, photo by Peter Maronn. **Page 8:** BGA. **Pages 9, 10, 11, 12:** *Ten Generations.* **Page 13:** courtesy Bristol Brass Corp. **Pages 14, 17, 18:** BGA. **Page 20:** *Ten Generations.* **Pages 21, 22:** BGA. **Pages 23, 24:** courtesy Peter Maronn. **Page 25:** *Ten Generations.* **Page 27:** courtesy The Downtown Café, Bristol, photo by Rick LaBranche. **Page 28:** BGA. **Page 29:** courtesy Hap Barnes. **Pages 30, 32, 33, 34, 35, 36:** BGA. **Page 37:** (top) courtesy Gary Freeland, NASCO; (bottom) BGA. **Page 38:** BGA. **Page 39:** courtesy Hap Barnes. **Pages 40, 41:** BGA. **Page 42:** courtesy Mrs. Edward Wozenski, photo by James R. Vann. **Page 43:** courtesy Bristol Public Library. **Pages 44, 45:** BGA. **Page 46:** from *The Pocumtuck,* Deerfield Academy, 1944. **Pages 48, 49, 50, 51, 52:** BGA. **Page 53:** photo by Rick LaBranche. **Pages 54, 55, 56:** BGA. **Page 57:** (left) courtesy Hap Barnes, (right) photo by Rick LaBranche. **Pages 59, 60:** BGA. **Page 61:** photo by Peter Maronn. **Page 62:** BGA. **Page 64:** BGA, photo by Rick LaBranche. **Page 65:** BGA. **Pages 66, 68:** photos by Rick LaBranche. **Pages 69, 70:** BGA. **Page 71:** photos courtesy Wally Barnes. **Page 72:** BGA. **Pages 73, 75:** photos by Rick LaBranche. **Pages 76, 77, 78:** BGA. **Page 80:** photo by Rick LaBranche. **Page 82:** BGA, photo by Mark J. Gaier. **Pages 83, 84, 85, 86:** photos by Rick LaBranche. **Pages 87, 91:** photos courtesy Flameco, NASCO.

The text of this book is set in Century Old Style, with Bauer Bodoni chapter titles. The paper is Centura Dull, 80 lb. Text.

Page numbers in Italics refer to illustrations and their captions.